unforeseen

ENDORSEMENTS

In her book, *Unforeseen*, Bailey Lynn is very vulnerable and shares stories to display how God has showed up in her life. I love her writing style and the reflection questions at the end of each chapter. If you need some encouragement and prompting to draw closer to God, this book is for you!

Leslie Speas

Author of *Confessions of a Hot Mess: From Mess to MESSage - 90 Days of Messages for the Hot Mess in You* and blogger at www.lesliespeas.com

Unforeseen is an authentically written book that deepens our walk with God as we learn from Bailey's keen ability to draw spiritual insight from unusual places. Bailey helps us see Jesus through her life's journey—whether breaking in a horse, being in a mirror maze, or dealing with a dog with pink eye. Readers will love reading and learning from the stories in this book as they find hope in the midst of their own unforeseen circumstances.

Heather Holleman

Author of *Seated with Christ: Living Freely in a Culture of Comparison*

Real, honest, and vulnerable, Bailey Lynn offers insight into the valleys of life and what to do when you find yourself in one. Through her soulful writing, Bailey affirms the realities of doubt, confusion, and unanswered questions when life hits hard and situations blindside you. Through Bailey's stories in *Unforeseen: Learning to Trust in God's Plan When Life Takes Unexpected Turns,* you can once again discover purpose and tools to restructure your perspective based on a scriptural foundation. You will be challenged with questions that only you can answer for yourself. This book is practical, inspiring, and deeply spiritual.

DeAnna Lynn Sanders

Author of *Unseen People: Sharing Light and Life with your Neighbors and the Nations*

BAILEY LYNN

A MEMOIR

unforeseen

LEARNING TO TRUST

IN GOD'S PLAN WHEN LIFE

TAKES UNEXPECTED TURNS

AMBASSADOR INTERNATIONAL
GREENVILLE, SOUTH CAROLINA & BELFAST, NORTHERN IRELAND

www.ambassador-international.com

Unforeseen

Learning to Trust in God's Plan When Life Takes Unexpected Turns
©2023 by Bailey Lynn
All rights reserved

Paperback ISBN: 978-1-64960-346-3
eISBN: 978-1-64960-363-0

Scripture quotations taken from The Holy Bible, English Standard Version. ESV® Text Edition: 2016. Copyright © 2001 by Crossway Bibles, a publishing ministry of Good News Publishers.

Edited by Martin Wiles
Cover design by Hannah Linder Designs
Interior typesetting by Dentelle Design

Scripture taken from the King James Version. Public Domain.

AMBASSADOR INTERNATIONAL
Emerald House Group, Inc.
411 University Ridge, Suite B14
Greenville, SC 29601
United States
www.ambassador-international.com

AMBASSADOR BOOKS
The Mount
2 Woodstock Link
Belfast, BT6 8DD
Northern Ireland, United Kingdom
www.ambassadormedia.co.uk

The colophon is a trademark of Ambassador, a Christian publishing company.

This book is dedicated to my mom. Thank you for being a constant reminder of how it looks to live the life of a godly woman. Your love and support through everything life has thrown my way has meant more to me than you could ever know.

"Life with God is not immunity from difficulties,
but peace within difficulties."

C.S. Lewis

TABLE OF CONTENTS

BEFORE YOU BEGIN

However this book ended up in your hands, I'm glad you are here. Before you dive in, there are some things I want to tell you.

This book is not designed as a devotional, so I recommend working through it at a pace that feels comfortable. Every chapter is another story or lesson God has placed on my heart to share. At the end of every chapter is a Bible verse or verses that provide a connection point from God's Word to the overarching theme of the chapter itself. I recommend locating those verses and reading the chapter. This will provide more context and help derive meaning from the message.

The chapters also end with a handful of reflection questions. I find it helpful to write down my answers to these questions in my journal. Feel free to approach these questions in the most comfortable way. Perhaps just read and consider each question in quiet time alone or work through them with a friend. Allowing God's Word to sink into our hearts is important.

Before I wrote each chapter, I prayed over them. Some dismiss prayer, but the power of prayer is so strong. I took seriously the responsibility of sharing the Word of God. I have prayed that these words will positively impact you and help you see more of who God is through the life experiences and stories I have included.

I also use a lot of metaphors. This is intentional. I love metaphors, especially when talking about God's kingdom because they make abstract concepts tangible. Spanish philosopher Jose Ortega y Gasset once said, "The metaphor is perhaps one of man's most fruitful potentialities. Its efficacy verges on magic, and it seems a tool for creation." Metaphors help us make meaningful connections in our minds. They have been studied in the disciplines of sociology, language, and even psychology as one of the most effective tools we can use to relate ourselves to others and the world.

Metaphors allow messages to resonate in us deeply. Let them sink in and wrestle with them in a way that creates meaning. Doing so helps us relate our experiences to the kingdom of God.

Unforeseen was never meant to be a book. After painful circumstances ended my engagement, I felt a sense of intense confusion and loneliness. The only way for me to fully get my thoughts out was to write. I felt as if I was at a fork in the road where I could choose bitterness and anger toward the Lord for the pain I was experiencing, or I could realize He could use it to refine and shape me to be more like Him. Through that experience, I learned about the true nature of God and experienced Him in ways I never had before. As I continued writing, I shifted away from the events leading up to a traumatic breakup and began writing about my walk with God in its entirety.

Some of the biggest things I continue to struggle with are distrust and control. I know God is faithful, but I often find myself afraid to give Him complete control. As I wrestled with this challenge, I continued to write. Pages piled up, and I realized my vulnerable experiences could help others. Although I have experienced many unique and sometimes crazy times, my life has continuously proven that Jesus is the only One with the ability to make our lives full and glorifying to Him. I have seen how more satisfying life can be when our mission is to glorify God instead of ourselves. The nature of Who God is has been revealed to me in amazing ways throughout my life's story.

Although God has taught me so much, I am far from perfect. Every day, I make mistakes that wedge a gap between me and the Lord. I am thankful for His mercy and grace that have allowed me to live in communion with Him, despite the ways I have failed. Yet I am broken. I don't have all the answers, and I don't always walk perfectly in step with God's plan. Rather, I come as a sister in Christ, excited for a chance to learn and grow in my faith with you.

I welcome you into my deepest and most real emotions. I hope that through a lot of my mistakes, a lot of my heartaches, and a lot of my unexpected circumstances, you will see the amazing ways God can work. I hope my experiences will help you give God control. Once we let Him call the shots, He will transform us in ways we never thought possible.

Chapter One

THE DRIVER'S SEAT

The section in Target where they sell planners is my kryptonite. I love planners. I could (and do) spend large amounts of money on planners—daily planners, monthly planners, work planners, social planners. It's kind of a weird thing, but it makes sense for me because it isn't the planner itself that I love having. It's the plan.

I love to check things off my planner when I am done with them and write new things in as I plan for them. It helps me feel as if I am taking the unknown out of the future. I like seeing what will come my way in the days, weeks, and months ahead. I know some people who are go-with-the-flow, free-spirit types. I'm glad for them. But I imagine many people are like me.

Some may not count perusing the planner aisle at the office supply store as a fun evening activity, but I think many people also appreciate having some of the ambiguity removed from the future.

Planning is in our nature. It's the reason we get stressed out when we are eighteen years old and haven't chosen a college major yet. It explains why we get frustrated with our flaky friend who just called to cancel plans for the third time in a row. We operate best when we know what to expect.

And while I don't think that planning is a bad thing, nor do I fault people for being uncomfortable with the unknown, I think we tend to over-plan. Our deep-rooted desire to know what the future holds can often kick God out of the driver's seat of our life. I know from experience—and the fact that God taught me this lesson the hard way several times—that the minute we put ourselves in the driver's seat, we begin heading toward a destination much worse than the place God was trying to take us when we trusted Him with the control.

Sometimes, God takes us down a winding road that seems dangerous and confusing. And sometimes, He has us make pit-stops in some less-than-scenic places. Through the disappointments and trials, we may wonder why we are taking this route at all. It looks unfamiliar; we don't understand the road signs; and we want to grab the phone and confirm there is an agreeable destination programmed into Apple Maps.

This book is for planners. For those of us who have every detail of our life written down in all three of our planners and typed into our Reminders app. For my friends who, like me, get uneasy when we can't see the destination. I know we think our destination is perfectly good and that we could probably drive there a lot quicker and smoother than anyone else.

But there is Someone Who wants to take us to a destination far better than the one we imagined. He knows the detours we must make and the things we need to pull over to view. He knows when we need to stop and refuel, as well as the best route to take to avoid dangerous conditions. This Driver's name is Jesus; and as difficult as it might be, we need to get in the passenger seat, buckle up, and let Him navigate.

The point of all of this is to walk through the ways we can lean on God and His Word when He takes us down a road we didn't anticipate. It is to describe how we can cope with all the thoughts and feelings that arise when we make pit stops in dangerous places that cause us to wind up a little wounded. It is to figure out how we can learn valuable lessons in all the seemingly unnecessary detours. Most importantly, it is to remind us of how more beautiful our destination will be (and how much more meaningful our road trip is) when we relinquish control and let God take the wheel.

In the Word:

"Trust in the Lord with all your heart, and do not lean on your own understanding. In all your ways acknowledge him, and he will make straight your paths" (Proverbs 3:5-6).

Reflection Questions:

- In what areas of my life do I struggle with letting God take the wheel? What parts of my life do I feel most comfortable managing on my own?
- How does the idea of letting God call the shots make me feel? Am I eager to slide into the passenger's seat, or is the thought of relinquishing control unsettling?

Chapter Two

PAINFUL PIT STOPS

When I met my ex-fiancé, I thought my lane and his had merged at the perfect time and in the perfect way. I thanked God that He had brought us together and that it seemed our destinations were the same. I thought, *I have found the person God intended for me to carpool with forever on a happy road toward His final destination for us as a couple.*

By my description of him as my ex-fiancé and the way I talk about our relationship in the past tense, it is apparent that this part of my story doesn't end with me in a white dress, walking down an aisle. In fact, it ended up with me in sweatpants, in the fetal position, crying my tear ducts dry while my dad held me in his arms.

My ex and I are both big planners. So naturally, we had planned our lives together down to the nitty-gritty details. Little, insignificant things like on what side of our future bed in our future home each of us would sleep. We had it all worked out. From my perspective, my life's plan was laid out, and everyone seemed on board with it. I thought I held the road map God was using to drive me, and I was excited about the places He would take me.

Three weeks after saying yes to an elaborately planned proposal, I stumbled across numerous text messages between my fiancé and his secret girlfriend. I trembled as I read through every message— the ones where he told her he wished he was with her and not me, the ones that recounted the romantic evenings the two of them had shared, and the ones that said hateful things about me.

I don't tell that story for anyone to feel sorry for me or to get mad at my ex. I tell it to illustrate the painful disruption to my plan. I thought God and I had agreed upon the itinerary for my journey. Now, suddenly, I found myself confused and angry with no clue how the map even looked—questioning if the Driver knew the best way to go.

My ex-fiancé and I spent our evenings long-distance over FaceTime doing devotionals and praying together. We had discussed the ministries we would commit ourselves to as a married couple and our desire to raise our kids to become God-fearing individuals. So, as I lay on my bed in tears and with a bare-naked left ring finger, my next question was why and how God could let it end like this.

I experienced a lot of sleepless nights and used many tissues before I came to terms with the reality of what had happened. Through all the doubt and anger I experienced after dealing with the initial shock, I realized God was not sitting idly by with His hands off the wheel as my car barreled toward a desolate and lonely place. Rather, He had His navigation set to take me to a painful pitstop I never saw coming. There, I would learn the most from Him.

In my time as a Christian, I have heard the following question often: "If God controls all things and is a God of love, why do bad things happen to us?" This is an insightful question. One that took a lot of painful experiences for me to understand, and one I still wrestle with when I walk through difficult times. But the answer is simple.

God is not "letting bad things happen to us" at all. He is not sitting in His recliner eating potato chips and watching us while we struggle and suffer. He is actively leading us into these difficult experiences. He makes us pull over and get out of the car in these dangerous and scary places so that we can learn lessons we can't learn on the freshly paved highway with the car in cruise control.

The psalmist said, "Even though I walk through the valley of the shadow of death, I will fear no evil, for you are with me; your rod and your staff, they comfort me" (Psalm 23:4).

This verse comes from a chapter that some Bible translations entitle, "The Lord Is My Shepherd." The chapter compares the Lord to a Shepherd Who cares for His sheep and goes to great lengths to protect them (that's the whole "rod and staff" part of this verse). Verse four is unique because unlike the other verses in the chapter, it discusses some less-than-pleasant scenarios the sheep must face.

Unlike the green pastures and still waters referenced in verse two, verse four talks about "the valley of the shadow of death." Napping in lush, green grass seems a lot more appealing than a hike through "the valley of the shadow of death." I would rather hang out with the verse two sheep and avoid the verse four ones at all costs.

I am from a suburban town in the Midwest. This lifestyle has resulted in limited interaction with sheep and limited knowledge about shepherding. The metaphor made in Psalm 23 between Jesus and the Shepherd isn't lost on me, however. I get the gist, but it leaves me with some questions. The biggest is that if we as sheep have access to the safe and soft, green pastures and get to take afternoon strolls by the still waters, why does the Shepherd make them walk through "the valley of the shadow of death"?

Many of the psalms were written by David, and he is clear on the kind of place this valley is. He could have been a little bit more subtle and referred to it as something less harsh. Perhaps "The Valley That's Kind of Scary." But he chose to name it "the valley of the shadow of death." We get it, David. The valley stinks. No one wants to go there.

But back to the question of why the Shepherd makes the sheep, who represent us, go to the creepy valley in verse four? W. Phillip Keller wrote a book entitled *A Shepherd Looks at Psalm 23*. He provides cool insight on this whole shepherd thing because he really *is* a shepherd and can fill in the holes my suburban upbringing has left. What he said in this book answers my question so beautifully.

The shepherd leads his sheep into the valley because there, they can get the best water that provides them with minerals and vitamins. Wow.

Let's apply our new knowledge. All the sheep must walk through the valley. The verse does not say, "If I walk through the valley." Nor does it say, "When I may have to consider walking through the valley because all the other paths are closed for maintenance." It says, "Even though I walk through the valley." We all *must* walk through the valley at some point. When we do, we can be sure the Shepherd has led us there because it is the place we are getting nutrients for our spirits that we cannot get anywhere else on the planet.

Is it scary to walk through the valley? Yep. Is it a long journey? Sometimes. Do we wish we were with our sheep buddies napping in the luscious pastures from verse two? One hundred percent. But we are being led to the valley because that is where we can get the best nourishment. And the whole time we are there, we are protected and comforted by the rod and staff of our Shepherd.

One of the deepest and darkest valleys I walked through was ending my engagement to the man I thought I was supposed to marry. I had to learn to let go of him, the dreams I had for us, and the security I had found in our detailed plan for the future. It was awful. King David was right in his description of that experience as being like walking in "the valley of the shadow of death." However, my experience in the depths of that valley taught me things and helped me grow in ways I never would have had I not passed through the valley.

Although the journey was difficult (and I mean, very difficult), the same Shepherd Who led me there also protected me from evil with His rod and staff.

Maybe you are in a valley right now, and the shadow of death is causing you to fear for your life. Perhaps you have just walked out of the valley, and the nutrients from the special valley water haven't quite kicked in, so you're questioning the point of the journey to the valley in the first place. Or maybe you're happily napping in the green paddock next to the still waters, and you don't even see a valley.

Rest assured that God, the Good Shepherd, uses our hardships to shape us into better versions of ourselves—versions of ourselves that result in us looking a little more like Him. Our Shepherd won't carelessly drag us through the valley without having His rod and staff handy to protect us. And when we come out of the valley, we will be nourished in ways we could not have dreamed had we comfortably rested in the pasture.

In the Word:

"The Lord is my shepherd; I shall not want. He makes me lie down in green pastures. He leads me behind still waters. He restores my soul. He leads me in paths of righteousness for his name's sake. Even though I walk through the valley of the shadow of death, I will fear no evil, for you are with me; your rod and staff, they comfort me" (Psalm 23:1-4).

Reflection Questions:

- What valleys have I had to walk through recently?
- Has walking through difficulties ever caused me to doubt God's ability to lead me?
- Where can I find joy in the valley? How does focusing on the positives in these hard times make it easier? Is focusing on the positive things difficult for me?
- What lessons might God be trying to teach me in these trials?

FOURTH DOWN

I understand the game of football, and I will watch it—provided I am with my friends, and someone sets out some chips and dip. But I am by no means a football expert, so bear with me.

Imagine the quarterback throws the ball to a wide receiver. As the receiver runs toward his team's end zone, ball tucked in his arm, a massive defender emerges from the side and throws the receiver onto his back.

The first time the wide receiver gets tackled for a first down, he's usually farther from his end zone and less likely to score points for his team in the next play. He is less of a threat to the defending team. When the offensive lineman takes the wide receiver down the first time, the wide receiver gets up relatively unharmed and plays again for a second down.

The team has four chances to get the ball into the end zone. With each play, they often get nearer their goal. But as they get closer to the end zone, the other team tackles them more aggressively. As they near the end zone, they pose a bigger threat to the defending team, and the defense must be more aggressive when taking down their opponents.

The game of football is like our relationship with Jesus when we are headed in the wrong direction. Sometimes, the devil throws us a ball and encourages us to run full force toward the wrong end zone. It breaks Jesus's heart when we run in the wrong direction, trying to score points for the wrong team. To protect us from heading in the wrong direction, Jesus tackles us. In my experience, the first down isn't an overly catastrophic take down for me, the receiver. More than anything, it is a warning from Jesus—a simple way to say, "Hey, you're running toward the wrong end zone."

I had a plan to take the ball to the end zone and score. I did not have enough foresight to see that the end zone belonged to the enemy's team or to learn from the first down that Jesus did not want me running that way. But being the bull-headed and determined competitor I am, I grab the ball again and run even farther down the field in the wrong direction. This cycle does not stop, though. Every play we make and every yard we inch closer and closer to the enemy's end zone, the closer we get to a rough take-down by God.

I learned this the hard way when I was planning my detailed and elaborate life with a man God never intended for me to marry. I ignored the warning signs from God. Determined to get the ball to the end zone, to start a life with the wrong man, I kept getting up and running a few more yards in the wrong direction. More than once, God blocked and tackled me. Early on, the injuries from His take-downs were never severe. Certainly not bad enough to stop me from playing. After I agreed to a proposal, God saw how close I was to reaching the wrong end zone. He tackled me so hard, I had to lie on the field with the wind knocked out of me for a long time.

Once I stood up, I saw I had suffered a few injuries. I would be on the sidelines for a while dealing with my pain and tending to my wounds. I realized then I was playing against the best Defense in the league. I should have known better after the first few tackles that it wasn't smart to keep running down the field with God in my way.

When we focus on the Lord, He reveals the direction He wants us to head and toward which end zone He wants us to run. And when we start heading the wrong way, He will try to stop us. Our actions don't mean we are strong-willed, though. We are planners who have set our minds on taking the ball toward the wrong end zone. We don't see a flaw in our plan, so we get up and keep running.

When God tackles us, He doesn't want to hurt us. Rather, He tries to protect us from running so far in the wrong direction that we end up scoring points for the wrong team.

The cool thing about God being an amazing linebacker, though, is that He offers us the opportunity to join His team. It is more fun running toward the end zone when we have the best defender in the league protecting us. When we and God agree over the right endzone, He will do what He does best and block the enemy's team from harming us. To decipher the next best play, sometimes we just need to go back to the locker room for a moment, take a break, and discuss the plan with our team.

When the best Defender has our backs, and we agree on the best plan of action, our team will be unstoppable. We won't make a touchdown every single play. And we will occasionally get knocked down by the other team's defense. But we'll find the game is more fun when we are playing on the winning team.

In the Word:

"The Lord is my rock and my fortress and my deliverer, my God, my rock, in whom I take refuge, my shield, and the horn of my salvation, my stronghold" (Psalm 18:2).

Reflection Questions:

- What areas of my life do I try to keep God from dictating? Why do I think my way is the best?
- How can I tell when I am running in the wrong direction?
- In what ways can I surrender to God and join His team?

Chapter Four

BREAKING IN A HORSE

When I was growing up, I loved horses. I went to the barn as much as possible and felt happiest when sitting in a saddle. I don't ride much anymore. My lifestyle as a full-time student and part-time employee leaves little spare time, but I still love the animal.

In high school, I rode with a woman named Jackie. She owned a lot of property and had a passion for rescue horses. She took horses from poor conditions, restored them to good health, and made them into "broke" horses. Broke horses are mild-tempered, and they are comfortable with people riding and working with them. Once a horse was broke, she would find it a permanent home.

Within a few months of meeting Jackie, she offered to let me come along to pick up horses from the rescue farm and bring them home. Soon enough, I began working with rescue horses, too. I fell in love with this process. Doing so is like flipping a house Chip and Joanna Gaines-style—except with horses.

These horses came from various scenarios, from retired racehorses to neglected pets. Every horse we picked up had varying comfort levels around people. Some, like the retired racehorses, did not mind having people around them or letting people ride them. We taught them the art of going slowly when they had a rider on their back. They were accustomed to sprinting their hearts out on the track. With just a little fine-tuning under the saddle and some medication for their sore joints, they were ready for adoption into their forever home.

Other horses, however, differed. Some, we had to wrestle just to get into the trailer. The thought of getting on their backs seemed like a dangerous idea that would probably cause us to end up in a bush with a broken bone or two. These horses were always my favorite. I loved watching their journey from being afraid of humans to going home with a family and being a pet for some little girl.

One horse's transition from start to end has stuck with me. He was strikingly beautiful. Tall and pristine white. But neglect had left him in bad shape. His hooves were misshapen; his fur was matted; and his ribs and hips protruded through his thin body. We named him Chase because just to get him out of the pasture, we had to run after him while he bolted in every other direction to avoid us. Sheer panic showed in his eyes every time a human neared him. He was distrusting and afraid.

Step one entailed restoring Chase to good health with proper grooming and nutrition. Step two involved teaching him to be comfortable around people. I had fun watching him figure out that people had food, and food was yummy. Eventually, when he would see me coming with a bucket of grain, he'd run to the fence line to greet me. Pretty soon, I didn't need the grain anymore. He ran over every time he saw me to say hi and get some pats. It was a big change from the horse that one month prior we named Chase because he did everything he could to avoid being near a human.

After a few weeks, he looked forward to bathing and grooming. He enjoyed people, and we started walking him around the yard with a saddle on his back to get him used to it. As he grew more and learned his ground manners, he was ready for a rider. I had grown attached to this animal, and naturally, I volunteered to be the first one on his back. I had done this many times with rescue horses, so when the day came for me to ride Chase for the first time, I was not overly fearful.

I led him over to the sand-filled arena and pulled a stepstool over to him so I could climb onto his back. He didn't like the step near him. This was my first indication he may not have been ready for a rider. Eventually, he let me sit on his back. I stroked his neck and told him he was a good boy just for allowing me in the saddle. Once we were both comfortable, I decided to ask him to walk forward.

Squeezing one's legs into a horse's side signals for them to go. As soon as I applied a little pressure, Chase took off like a watermelon seed pinched between a thumb and an index finger. I used the reins to pull him back and navigate him; but he had taken off like a rocket, and it didn't seem as if he planned to touch down anytime soon. I held on as he ran, but his main goal was to get me off him. I was a sixteen-year-old girl; he was a two-thousand-pound animal. He won the disagreement.

With panic in his eyes, Chase planted his front legs in the sand and threw his back legs up into the sky until I couldn't hold on any longer. I ended up with my face in the dirt. He ended up as far away from me as possible.

When I was a teenager, I was stubborn and stupid. Instead of protecting myself from the possibility of a head injury, I tried again the next day. Chase was still traumatized from the day before, so he didn't want me near him. Although I knew he was terrified, I got on anyway.

We passed the point of my praising him for letting me climb on and reached the point where I had to ask him to move again. Neither of us looked forward to it, but it had to happen. I gently applied pressure to his sides and asked him to step. He moved forward into a big, lofty trot. It was awkward and uncomfortable, but at least he didn't try to get rid of me. We didn't look graceful, but for the first time, he trusted me to call the shots.

I worked with Chase every day, and with time, he loved going to the ring for rides. He trusted me to take the reins and use them to lead him through different exercises. On a few occasions, I even took him to horse shows. We never did well, but I was proud he could even compete, given all he had experienced.

Jackie's farm was near a cider mill, which is where they press apples to make cider and serve fresh donuts during autumn in the Midwest. That fall, I rode Chase to the cider mill with my friends and their horses. We ate donuts, drank cider, and fed the horses apples from the Michigan apple trees. Chase loved the cider mill, but he would never have gone had he not learned to trust me to control the reins. The process involved a big learning curve and a few instances where I ate dirt. Ultimately, he was broken in enough to get adopted into his forever home. His new owner was a sweet, older widow. She gave us updates occasionally, and she treated Chase as if he was a king.

When I think about the experience I had with Chase, I can't help but think of my walk with the Lord. Especially when it comes to thinking I know the best course of action for myself. I reluctantly allow God to take the reins in my life and steer me in a direction I had not intended to go. I have thrown God off my back several times and left Him in the dirt while I ran the other way—all because I did not trust His ability to lead me in the right direction.

What is so awesome about God is that He is a lot like me as a stubborn teenager with no fear of injuring my spinal cord. When we ditch Him and take off in our own direction, He continues to pursue us and get back in our saddle day after day. The more we allow God to take the reins in our lives, the more we realize He is a trustworthy rider. Getting used to having God lead us takes practice. But the more we are willing to open ourselves to His direction, the more we will work as a team and accomplish amazing things.

In the Word:

> "I will instruct you and teach you in the way you should go;
> I will counsel you with my eye upon you" (Psalm 32:8).

Reflection Questions:

- When have I tried to throw God off my back and run away from Him?
- In what ways have I tried to rebuild trust with God and give Him back control?
- Where can God take me when I trust Him to take me where I cannot go on my own?

Chapter Five

THIS SEASON

I have written a lot so far on how God will take us through difficulties as part of His plan for our life. We know we will likely endure difficulties, but how do we handle them? How we carry ourselves when we are walking through trials is something Jesus talks a lot about in the Bible, and it's an area we can miss the mark on quite a bit.

Have you ever noticed home décor and craft stores rarely sell items for the season in which we shop? We can walk into Michael's in July and be bombarded with Halloween décor. Then once Halloween does roll around, all the Halloween décor is on a clearance rack hidden behind red and green ornaments and knit stockings.

I am a lot like the craft store in this way. Over-planners can probably relate. We are never totally comfortable in the season we are in. We are forward thinkers, constantly looking ahead to the next thing and planning for what the future may bring.

The issue with obsessing over what's next, though, is that we forget a reason exists for this season. God brought us to this stage of life with our current circumstances to teach us something. I am the first one to admit that I am guilty of ignoring the season of life I am in because I am so focused on what's next. But the truth is that when we don't allow ourselves to settle into this season, we miss what

God is teaching. I can't learn the lesson He wants to teach me on the fourth of July if I am focused on preparing for Halloween.

Not every season of our life is beautiful. I am from Michigan, and I am not a big fan of Michigan summers. They are kind of muggy and too hot for me. I get excited for the leaves to change to their beautiful autumn colors, and I finally get to bust out my extensive sweater collection. As much as I wish I could, however, I can't hit fast forward on the summer and jump right into pumpkin spice season.

Our walk with God is similar. Sometimes, the rain and humidity make our hair frizzy, and we can't escape the heat. God asks us to lean into this discomfort because the season of life we are in is an intentional part of our journey. We can't appreciate the beauty of a Michigan autumn if we never endure the hot and humid days that came just a few months earlier.

I realized my struggle with this right after I accepted the situation that had ended my engagement. There was a time when my heart and mind were prepared for marriage. I was ready for the next chapter of my life to start. The season of my life where I was single was ending. But just like that, the metaphorical groundhog saw his shadow, and the season of singleness I found myself in was extended.

There I was—fiancé-less, wondering why I was back in this season of my life when I was so excited for the next one. In fact, I had thought I was already in the next one, but it turned out to be a random cool day in the middle of the still-hot summertime. Once I came to grips with what had happened, I pulled a classic craft-store move and fixated on the next season again.

I panicked because I was uncomfortable with the stage of life in which I was. My poor mother has had to listen to endless rants of my worry.

"I am never going to be engaged again." "Where am I supposed to find a man that I want to marry?" "Now I am all alone."

But I realized God did not bring me into this season of singleness just for me to panic and fixate on marriage and a family all over again. He brought me here because I had lessons in this season of my life I could not learn in other seasons. Singleness is a gift from God, but it is not viewed that way by the world. An abundance of opportunities has come with the season I am in that would not have if I was married.

Maybe your season is not singleness. Perhaps you are battling illness for yourself or a loved one. God needs you to learn things through this suffering that He can't teach you with good health. Maybe you are struggling to get pregnant, and you can't understand why you aren't able to have children. There are experiences you can have independently that you cannot have once you're a parent.

Whatever it may be, there is always beauty in the season we are in when we try to see it. When all we want to do is plan for the next season and prepare for what is around the corner, we need to learn to be comfortable in the season God has us. God has something for us to learn and grow from.

Although they are a little humid and a tad too hot, Michigan summers have plenty to do that I can't do in any other season. Whether it's kayaking on the local lake, enjoying the seasonal roadside ice cream shop, or relaxing by the pool, beauty resides during the season. As much as I can't wait for autumn, if I spent the whole summer inside my house, harboring Halloween decorations, I would miss the beauty of the summer. The art of learning to trust God and absorb the beauty of the season makes each season we pass through more meaningful.

Whether we read the Bible over and over or never spent time in God's Word, we have probably heard something about Jesus' time on earth. Whether it was turning water into wine, walking on water, or rising from the dead, His public ministry in the Bible is the most legendary biography ever written. Its popularity today, thousands of years after His life, testifies to how impactful His life was. But Jesus' public ministry was only three years.

In three years, Jesus did the majority of what the Gospels record . . . and more. Made a blind man see and a lame man walk. Fed five thousand people with only five loaves of bread and two fish. Walked on water and rose from the dead. From about age twelve to age thirty, we don't know a lot about Jesus's time on earth. He worked as a carpenter and waited for His season to begin.

I don't know about Jesus, but if it was me, I think the waiting would have been difficult. I think I would have prayed to God a lot and wondered why I had spent the last decade and a half hanging drywall if I had been sent to save humanity. Of course, Jesus had some ministry presence in those early years, but He needed to continue to grow.

But in those years before His ministry began, Jesus was in a season of preparation for the work He was about to do for God's kingdom. Jesus patiently waited on God's perfect timing so that His work could be done.

We might see this in our lives. It is easy, in such times, to question our purpose. We might wonder why we are waiting or walking through difficulty or doing something that we don't feel is our calling. In those seasons, God works through us. He refines and prepares us to be even better vessels through which Him can work. Just like Jesus in the nearly two decades He spent waiting for His public ministry to begin, the season we find ourselves in today is where God wants us.

We can have peace in God's perfect timing if we remain faithful to Him within those periods when it feels difficult. Steadfast is the word the Bible uses to describe our faithfulness to God during difficult seasons.

Naomi, in the book of Ruth, is a good example. She and her husband, Elimelech, lived in Bethlehem with their two sons. Because of a famine, her family decided to relocate to a city called Moab. Naomi's boys met women in Moab whom they married. Naomi's new daughters-in-law were named Ruth and Orpah.

Elimelech and his two sons died, leaving Naomi, Ruth, and Orpah as widows. Hearing that the famine in Bethlehem was over, Naomi and Ruth returned to Naomi's home. Orpah stayed in Moab with her family. When Naomi returned to Bethlehem, a bunch of her old pals recognized her and said, "Hey, Naomi! Long time, no see. What's up, girl?" (I am paraphrasing just a tad here.)

The name Naomi means "sweet and pleasant"; but after fleeing her home because of the drought and famine, suffering the loss of her husband and both sons, and voyaging back to her home with only one of her two daughters-in-law, Naomi didn't identify with the whole sweetheart vibe anymore.

These women lived in a time when a woman's mission in life was to marry and have babies. Both Ruth and Naomi were heartbroken after the loss of their husbands. Suddenly, they were faced with the reality that they may never be able to carry on their family's lineage. This broke Naomi's heart. In response to her old friend's greeting, she goes into a tangent: "Do not call me Naomi; call me Mara, for the Almighty has dealt very bitterly with me. I went away full, and the LORD has brought me back empty. Why call me Naomi, when the Lord has testified against me and the Almighty has brought calamity upon me?" (Ruth 1:20-21).

I can only imagine the face of the person on the receiving end of this little rant. She didn't say this exactly, but I imagine she thought something along the lines of "Woah, I just said hi to be nice. Wasn't really looking for your life story."

Naomi lived in Bethlehem and ranted to random people about how she was kind of a hot mess, and then her daughter-in-law Ruth met this guy named Boaz. Boaz married Ruth and helped her and Naomi in their unfortunate circumstance. Boaz and Ruth then carried on the family lineage and cared for Naomi in her old age. From the lineage of Naomi came King David and eventually Jesus. After all of this hurt and distrust and bitterness, Naomi became King David's grandma.

Naomi realized God had been working this whole time, and the whole story ends with these blessings and newfound joy coming from a difficult season of trials.

Her story applies today because it reminds us that godly people aren't exempt from difficult situations in life. However, blessings will come when we are steadfast through uncomfortable seasons. Naomi was not a perfect example—she became bitter and angry with the Lord. We can learn from her mistakes and remain confident in God's plan for our lives even through trials. That is the epitome of steadfastness.

I wish I could say I was faithful and patient in my season of unexpected singleness and that I am now happily engaged to a godly man. I wasn't, and I'm not. But I am learning to lean into the discomfort of the season, as well as the unknown of the seasons to come. Noticing the beauty of this season has allowed God to work through me in ways He could not have had I focused on the next season.

In the Word:

"Blessed is the man who remains steadfast under trial, for when he has stood the test he will receive the crown of life, which God has promised to those who love him" (James 1:12).

Reflection Questions:

- What season of life am I in now? What are the difficult aspects associated with this season?

- Why might God have me in this season? What can I learn from this season?

- How can I see the positive through the difficulties I am facing?

- In what ways can I prepare my heart for the future without ignoring the lessons God wants me to learn from my present circumstances?

Chapter Six

MIRROR MAZES

Okay, so you let God sit in the driver's seat, let Him take the reins, joined His football team, and trusted His plan for your life. Now what? This is a question I wrestled with a lot the first time I allowed God to have total control of my future. And I still struggle with this daily.

God does not care about your Google calendar. He doesn't add in events so all we must do is check the app and say, "Okay, so I see in three months, You have me doing this thing I didn't expect. I trust You though, God, so let's do it." That would be cool and helpful, but that is not how God communicates His plans. So, how does God communicate His plans?

Many times, we don't know where to go. Even when we trust God, it can be difficult to know the right direction, but there are a few ways we can know where He wants us to go.

When my brothers and I were kids, our family was close with a couple at our church. This couple had three kids who were about our same age. We hung out with them quite a bit. One time, we took a trip with them to a place called Wheels Inn in Ontario, Canada. We grew up near Detroit, so Canada was a fairly quick trip.

Wheels Inn was like a giant resort mecca for families. It had a water park, arcade, tennis courts, and a bowling alley. It was like childhood heaven. We hung out, being kids and enjoying what we thought was a little taste of heaven on earth.

The resort had a maze with walls of mirrors. I'm not sure they let kids in those things anymore because they were a concussion waiting to happen. My brothers and I, along with the three kids from the other family, decided it would be fun to do the mirror maze. Mirror mazes are horribly disorienting. Three walls are made of mirrors, and the fourth opens to the next part of the maze, but all the sides look the same. The entire experience is confusing for a kid. The best way to get through a mirror maze is to walk toward what is believed to be an opening. Sometimes, it is the opening, but sometimes, it's a mirror, which means rerouting.

All six of us were in the mirror maze, and everyone took a cautious approach, walking slowly with our arms extended so we could detect if we were at an opening or a mirror. This technique worked well. Once someone advanced through an opening, they informed the others, and we all followed. We did well until Eric, the youngest son from the other family, got a little too confident.

"Guys, it's this way!" he called as he ran toward what he thought was an opening. He ran face-first into a mirror. This happened a long time ago, but to this day, I remember the noise his face made hitting the glass followed by the wail he let out. At this point, he needed his mom, but it had taken us twenty minutes to get that far. It would take the same amount of time to return the way we came. His best option was to pick himself up and head toward the end goal.

Eric is fine. Don't worry. We no longer talk; but I follow him on Instagram, and he makes amazing videos and is musically talented. He has made a full recovery from the mirror maze incident of 2007.

But his unfortunate event at Wheels Inn years ago is still memorable because of the way it symbolizes trusting God's plan.

The best way to navigate life is to make the next obvious move forward. If we stand still and wait for direction, we may never progress. Once we are moving, if we are fixing our eyes on the Lord, He will guide us where we need to go. Sometimes, a mirror looks a lot like an open door, and we pull an Eric and crash into it. God never promises He will shield us from bumping into walls. He uses our mirror-crash moments to show us we have not headed the right way.

What is so cool about God is that as long as we are fixated on Him, He offers us a little direction through this disorienting maze we call life. We don't have to walk blindly and hope we don't face-plant into a mirror.

Another way God speaks to us is through the voices of other godly people. Seeking and surrounding ourselves with other people who are also walking with the Lord is an amazing way to find out in which direction we're supposed to head. The kicker is that when godly people try to offer us advice, we should take their opinions seriously.

I don't tell him this enough, but I look up to my oldest brother, Bryce, in so many ways. He is an incredible embodiment of what it looks like to walk along the path the Lord has laid out. I watch him put on the armor of God every day in his work with the U.S. Navy and his home life with his beautiful wife and daughter.

When I first discussed my engagement with Bryce, he expressed some valid concerns. I was—and still am—stubborn. I had decided I wanted to be engaged, and I did not want to take Bryce's opinions seriously. I didn't listen to him and was even angry that he voiced any opinion other than complete joy and acceptance of my decision.

I am not saying we need to take every piece of advice from every Christian and use it to guide our lives. Some advice is bad, and while it should be respected, it does not mean we need to always follow it. Discretion and wisdom are needed. However, finding people who love the Lord and us can help us find direction along the right path.

Sometimes, humbling ourselves enough to listen to someone's advice—even when we disagree with it—can save us from a lot of hurts and potential face-plants into mirrors. God often uses those important people for our good. If you hear advice from someone who has your best interests at heart, but you don't like the advice, take a minute to consider what they are saying and don't be so quick to disregard them.

In addition to taking the next obvious step forward and seeking advice from godly people who want the best for us, we can also decipher God's plan by utilizing our gifts and passions. He has designed each of us with unique gifts and abilities that we can use to glorify Him. The most beautiful thing is to watch someone combine their earthly passions with their heavenly purpose.

My dad is a doctor. Since I was a little girl, I have always loved watching my dad go above and beyond to take care of his patients. I wanted to grow up and be just like him. I would tell anyone who asked that I was going to grow up and work with my dad. His office had a back room where they kept the paper charts. No one in medicine uses paper charts anymore, so the room of old patient records was virtually useless. Naturally, that is where I chose to set up my office.

I would go to work with my dad when I was young and decorate the chart closet with Bailey's Office signs. I used an old table as my desk, and I had my own collection of pencils and a little schedule of fake patients.

The passion to work in medicine was prominent in my heart even when I was a little kid. I took that passion and began working toward becoming a health care provider. Getting to care for patients is a privilege for me, and it provides opportunities to share the good news of the Gospel with my patients and to represent Christ.

What I love about the community of Christians is that God has given each of us unique passions so we can work together to reach as many people as possible. The church is often referred to as the body of Christ, and He is the Head. But we wouldn't work well if we were all the same organs. We can't all be pastors much in the same way that our entire body can't be a liver. If we follow our earthly passion, God will assign us a heavenly purpose, and collectively, we can combine those to bring Him glory.

Life is full of mirrors. Many good opportunities present themselves, but God often heads us in a different direction. Although it can be frustrating at times and we might bruise our foreheads now and again, we cannot stop pursuing the path the Lord wants us to take.

Some people give up, and many stand there pounding on a mirror because they are convinced it should be a door. If we as Christians learn from the times that we bump into the mirrors and continue to look for open doors instead, we will come out on the other side of the maze with a promise of eternity spent with our Heavenly Father. We can get through the maze by listening to the advice of Christian people who have gone through it before us.

Our passions and talents are a gift from God that can provide us with direction. And sometimes, when we're standing in the mirror maze, frustrated that every wall looks just like a door, we simply need to walk forward and see where God takes us. And if we bump our heads, we're likely heading in the wrong direction. Turn around and look for the open door.

In the Word:

> "Now may the God of peace who brought again from the dead our Lord Jesus, the great shepherd of the sheep, by the blood of the eternal covenant, equip you with everything good that you may do his will, working in us that which is pleasing in his sight, through Jesus Christ, to whom be glory forever and ever" (Hebrews 13:20-21).

Reflection Questions:

- What path am I trying to pursue? Am I inviting God to guide me through the maze of life?
- Are there obstacles in my way that won't seem to move? Might this be an indication that I am headed in a direction that is different than the way God wants me to move?
- Who do I have whose opinion I value the most? Do they love me and want my life to glorify God?

Chapter Seven

MELTED GOLD

I, like many other girls, always dreamed of the perfect engagement ring. I had a Pinterest board that began in the sixth grade where I saved photos of rings I loved. When it finally came time for my ex-fiancé and me to look at rings, I was excited. I had always wanted a pear-shaped, yellow-gold ring. When he got down on one knee at sunrise in front of a beautiful Michigan lighthouse and opened the ring box, I was blown away by how beautiful the ring was. It was exactly what I had dreamed about since I was a little girl.

But the way I felt about the ring had a lot less to do with the ring itself than with what the ring represented. Although it was gorgeous, I thought it was perfect because it represented the love and commitment my fiancé and I shared.

When everything that the ring represented was taken away, the ring shifted from the most beautiful thing I had ever seen to a painful reminder that brought me to tears every time I looked at it. Letting go of that ring was the first step toward healing because it represented letting go of the love, commitment, and future the ring symbolized.

I had taken the ring to a few jewelers to have it appraised because I planned to sell it. The jewelers all told me the same thing: "We just want it for parts. We will take the diamonds out, put them into different rings, and melt down the gold to make a different piece of jewelry."

At first, this confused me. I thought it was the most amazing piece of jewelry in the world. Why wouldn't someone want it the way it was? But as I thought more about my ring, I realized it made perfect sense that the jewelers wanted it for parts. The ring represented the love and commitment my ex-fiancé and I had made to one another. No one wants a symbol of my love story; they want a unique ring to represent their own.

Letting go of the ring was difficult, but envisioning it being destroyed was worse. On the night I had gotten rid of my ring, I ate dinner with my brother and sister-in-law. As I explained the hurt I felt after saying goodbye to the ring and all it represented, my sister-in-law started talking about the process of smelting and refining gold. She told me that when jewelers melt gold, they must use intense heat so that all the impurities will rise to the top. The jeweler then scrapes the impurities off the top and continues to heat and refine the gold until it is so pure that he can see his reflection in it.

This is what had happened to me. Much like my ring, I represented something different than what God wanted. I thought I was okay the way I was, but I didn't realize the shape God wanted me to embody was much different and better than the shape I was in before. To shape me into the form He envisioned, He had to melt me. I had to endure incredible heat and discomfort so He could reduce me to a material with which He could work. He turned the heat up so high that it exposed all my impurities. During this extreme discomfort and pain, God scraped the impurities off me so He could see His reflection in my life.

My engagement ended abruptly when we were visiting friends in Cincinnati. My ex and I argued, talked, questioned, and cried about the hurtful and unexpected conclusion to our relationship until the early hours of the morning. Unable to sleep, I packed my things and drove to my parents' house in Detroit at seven a.m. I was sleep-deprived, shocked, and heartbroken. As I drove north on I-75, I heard the song "New Wine" by Hillsong. The lyrics hit me in a new way as they spoke of a person asking God to make them whatever He wanted them to be.

I broke down. For the first time in my life, I had been crushed and pressed down. Everything I thought was important was taken from me, and the only thing I had left was Jesus. On that highway in the early morning, I raised my hands to the Lord and invited Him to rebuild my brokenness in whatever way He thought was best. I asked Him to melt my metal, remove my impurities, and make me into a piece of jewelry more beautiful than before.

Inviting the Lord into our broken and desperate moments allows us the opportunity to surrender our plans to Him. When our expectations are shattered and our plans change in a way we never saw coming, God has a raw piece of metal to reform into a person that is more like Him. Trusting God to use our brokenness for His glory is one of the most beautiful opportunities we have as Christians.

Wherever you are, ask God to turn up the heat on your life. The process is incredibly painful. Being melted down to nothing, allowing our impurities to be exposed, and then having them scraped off our lives is an uncomfortable experience. But afterward, we will be such a shiny piece of jewelry that we will reflect the face of Jesus to anyone who looks at us. That makes the refining process worth our while.

In the Word:

"And we all, with unveiled face, beholding the glory of the Lord, are being transformed into the same image from one degree of glory to another. For this comes from the Lord who is the Spirit" (2 Corinthians 3:18).

Reflection Questions:

- Are there things in my life I value so much that I am afraid to give to God? Might these things be idols in my life? How can I make sure a relationship with Jesus is the most valuable thing in my life?

- What does refinement mean to me? What might it look like in my life?

- How do I feel about asking God to turn up the heat and expose my impurities?

- Have I been melted down or crushed in any way lately? How can I allow God to use my experiences?

Chapter Eight

STORM PREPARATION

I love to tell stories. Drawing meaning from the stories in my life helps me see God working. This story, however, is not my story. But I want to retell it because of the lessons we can learn from it.

My parents are sailors. They have some close friends who also enjoy sailing and had purchased a sailboat. My parents and their friends keep their boats together in the same marina. These friends have a daughter who is my age, and we are close friends.

In Detroit, we have many large lakes, including the beautiful Lake Saint Clair, where a lot of local people sail and speedboat during the summer months. One summer day, my dad had been on the water with some people from the marina. They spent the morning racing their sailboats. As the day progressed, the wind picked up, and it seemed a storm might blow in. The conditions made sailing difficult and somewhat dangerous, so my dad and his crewmates decided to head back to the marina.

As they traveled back to the marina, they passed their friends taking their brand-new boat out to the water with my good friend aboard.

"The winds are pretty bad," my dad warned them as they passed one another.

But excited about breaking in their new boat, they were determined, so they decided to continue through the canal toward the lake. As they sailed, the waves got taller, and the high winds tossed their boat around. They quickly found controlling their boat was difficult and dangerous in that kind of weather.

Lake Saint Clair is deep, but boaters need to know of certain shallow areas. With their long rutters, sailboats can get stuck in them. As the wind and waves tousled our friends, their rutters became stuck on the lake's floor. One of the people aboard the boat had climbed into the cabin during all this chaos. To make a bad situation worse, she discovered the engine had caught on fire. Smoke filled the cabin.

There they were, stuck in the middle of the lake on a new sailboat with no engine and an aggressive storm. My friend who was aboard the boat flagged down a larger boat nearby. When the owners of the bigger boat approached, my friends explained their precarious situation. The people on the big boat informed my friends they couldn't tow them, but they could give them the number of the boat towing company. Of course, they took the rescue number, called the boat towing company, and were safely towed back to the marina. Everyone on board was shaken up but otherwise okay.

As I listened to my friend retell this story from her point of view, she said something that stuck with me: "Not only did we sail in the middle of a storm, but we also sailed with no emergency phone numbers."

When we live without Jesus, we can get ourselves into situations like the sailboat in the storm. Storms are inevitable. But when we ignore the advice of people who tell us not to enter the channel and we find ourselves thrown around by the waves, we always have a number to call for help.

Maintaining an active prayer life is critical. Prayer is the phone number of the tow company. We cannot make it back to shore without Jesus, and we don't want to test His number for the first time when our engine is on fire, the winds are howling, and our boat is stuck on the lake's floor. When we are accustomed to daily conversations with Jesus, we get better at hearing His voice even when it's windy.

Another way to prepare for these storms is through regular time in God's Word. The sixty-six books of the Bible teach us how to use God as an anchor to hold us steady when the waves get high and the winds of our life blow strongly.

But prayer is not meant to be an emergency hotline only. And the Bible is not an emergency manual to use exclusively in desperate situations. God intends for us to use these tools regularly so that when the storm comes, we are already familiar with the equipment necessary to survive and even thrive in the storms.

As our earthly relationships are unique and different, our relationship with our Heavenly Father is not a one-size-fits-all either. Although these are the practices that make the most sense in my life, all people need to find a routine that works in their pursuit of a deeper relationship with God.

I am a morning person. I value time with Jesus before I start my day and spend it reading His Word, praying, and worshipping Him. For me, starting my day with Jesus is the best way to make sure God is my number one priority. Before my feet hit the ground, I pray and thank God for another day.

I grab a cup of coffee and get right into God's Word. I like to read along with a devotional or spend time reading the same chapters in the Bible as my spiritual role models do. I look up to the relationship my sister-in-law, Kortney, has with Jesus. I like to read what she reads in the Bible so we can discuss and challenge each other.

When I spend time in God's Word, I make sure it is only Jesus and me. Although I love a good Instagram story with a steaming cup of coffee, an open Bible, and a cute, lit candle in the corner, I know it's more important to put my phone away and focus on Jesus. Not doing so is like going to dinner with friends and messing on the phone. Have you ever seen people at restaurants, but they're all on their phones and not talking with each other? I've been guilty of this. Why set aside time to spend with someone if we're focused on social media? We need to put our phones away and focus on cultivating the relationship in front of us.

As I get ready for the day—whether I'm putting away dishes, making my breakfast, or curling my hair—I spend a few minutes listening to worship music. Praising Jesus through music is one of my favorite things, and I love it when I get a good worship song stuck in my head. All day, I can repeat the truth of the Gospel.

The last thing I do is a new practice that is simple yet transformative. When I pray at night and in the morning, I kneel before the Lord. This action was semi-awkward at first, but physically kneeling and humbling ourselves as we talk to God is one of the best ways I have found to talk to Him. It helps me focus on my conversation with my Heavenly Father and show Him my respect and love for Him.

These are practices I use to maintain my relationship with God, but they are not universal. Try them out and see what works for you. Daily time spent strengthening our relationship with God should be the most important part of every day.

We can go onto the lake with no experience using these emergency tools, but those who have prepared for the storm through constant prayer and devotion have anchored themselves in God's Word and will find the storm much easier to weather.

In the Word:

> "Everyone then who hears these words of mine and does them will be like a wise man who built his house on the rock. And the rain fell, and the floods came, and the winds blew and beat on that house, but it did not fall, because it had been founded on the rock. And everyone who hears these words of mine and does not do them will be like a foolish man who built his house on the sand. And the rain fell, and the floods came, and the winds blew and beat against that house, and it fell, and great was the fall of it" (Matthew 7:24-27).

Reflection Questions:

- What is the current state of my prayer life? Is talking to God something I am comfortable with, or do I feel as if I need to improve my communication with Him?

- Am I anchored in Christ so that if the storms come, I won't be blown over?

- Are prayer and time in God's Word daily parts of my life? How can I implement these practices into my life to make sure I am prepared for any storm that may come?

Chapter Nine

A DOG WITH PINK EYE

When I turned eighteen, I did what nearly every person looks forward to doing on their eighteenth birthday: not voting or purchasing lottery tickets but adopting a dog. I lived in Southern Ohio at the time, and, after looking at hundreds of dogs on the internet, I found a little Jack Russell/Beagle mix in Kentucky who stole my heart.

He was at a shelter located about forty-five minutes from where I lived; so, on my birthday, I wrangled up one of my roommates, and we drove to pick him up. The no-kill shelter he lived at named him Dusty because when they found him, he was covered in dirt and dust.

I thought that was an unfortunate name, so I renamed him Beau. Beau was about thirty pounds, and he was white with orangish-brown polka dots. Beau is a ridiculously cute little critter, and he's been my little buddy for three years.

As of this writing, he is five years old. Since I adopted him, we have become a package deal. I have morphed into one of those people who are way too much into their dogs. Like those people who make their dogs scrambled eggs in the morning and maintain an Instagram account for them. It's embarrassing, but true.

Once, I dog-sat for my brother and sister-in-law while they backpacked in Northern Michigan. They had two pit bulls named Zoe and Moose. Zoe was less than a year old, and she was kind of a spaz. I had their dogs along with Beau for a week. A few days into dog-sitting, I looked at Zoe and noticed her eyes were red and goopy. My next thought was that she had pink eye.

The next morning, I looked at Moose and realized his eyes were also red and goopy. Then I saw Beau, and his eyes were so infected, they were swollen shut. It was a nasty image. I am kind of a crazy dog mom, so seeing Beau with pink eye upset me a lot. I got prescription eye drops to administer to all three dogs. Zoe and Moose had milder cases, but Beau's was by far the worst.

Despite having the worst case of pink eye, Beau was the least compliant with his eye drop regimen. I had to put them in every two hours, which was especially neat considering I worked full time and spent about two hours just to get a drop in one eye (I'm exaggerating a bit but not by much). The whole experience was quite an ordeal.

Beau is not aggressive, but he is a super big scaredy-cat. When I approached him with the drop bottle, he growled and hid under the table. I tried everything, from sedating him to tackling him to using the element of surprise. The majority of the drops ended up on the floor.

What I found somewhat helpful was putting the drops into a mini squirt gun and shooting them into his eye when he least expected it. And I'm not even exaggerating. He was so mad, he growled at me and ran away. I could only treat one eye at a time.

This whole ordeal frustrated me. I could see he was in pain, and I had the treatment. Pink eye can't heal on its own. Although the drops scared him, I needed him to trust me to administer them. Couldn't he see I was doing this out of love and that I knew what was best?

I love Beau, but he is a dog and not super intelligent. I am not a genius, but I know a little more than he does. When I looked like a complete idiot, chasing him around with a little squirt gun filled with eye drops wondering why he didn't understand I was trying to help him, I realized this is how I act with Jesus.

Sometimes, we don't realize how infected our lives are. And if we do notice, we are pretty sure we can take care of it on our own. When Jesus tries to offer treatment for our illnesses through His Word, we run from Him, hide, and growl.

Although God's treatment is scary, He intervenes because He has the remedy. We tend to act like Beau—distrust and fear God's intervention. Also, like Beau, we aren't always smart enough to realize God knows what is best. He loves us so much, He will put us through things that frighten us to make us better.

Trusting is one of the major keys to allowing God to have total control. We need to get accustomed to Him putting us through difficult and scary situations. He knows we need these experiences to make us better. God has the prescription to treat the infections that consume our lives. As much as we think we can treat it ourselves, He is the only way we can be healed. Every other remedy is a temporary Band-Aid that may bring relief but cannot fully rid us of the illness. We need to stop running and welcome God's intervention.

In the Word:

> "O Lord, by these things men live, and in all these is the life of my spirit. Restore me to health and make me live! Behold, it was for my welfare that I had great bitterness; but in love you have delivered my life from the pit of destruction, for you have cast all my sins behind your back" (Isaiah 38:16-17).

Reflection Questions:

- Are there areas of my life that are infected? In what aspects of my life do I struggle with sin?
- Do I struggle to allow God into the aspects of my life and acknowledge that He has the remedy for my infection?

Chapter Ten

THE DISNEY MYTH

I am a sucker for Disney movies. I love to know what the future holds. While each Disney movie is unique in its adorable way, each one is predictable. That is the reason I love them.

The beautiful princess with the incredible singing voice always rides into the sunset, holding the hand of a dashingly handsome prince. Flynn Rider and Rapunzel. Anna and Kristoff. Cinderella and Prince Charming. Each of their stories can be concluded with the phrase, "And they lived happily ever after." These stories are comforting. These resolutions are why I and millions of others are drawn to them.

My favorite Disney story has always been *Beauty and the Beast.* I could watch the live-action rendition starring Emma Watson repeatedly and never get bored. I love that Belle is independent, smart, and courageous. She saw something in the Beast that no one else saw. She looked beyond the outward appearance of the Beast and got to know his character. They fell in love and, of course, lived happily ever after.

We are fed these neat stories wrapped up with a bow from the time we are kids. I found myself craving this kind of perfect story for my own life. When I reflected on why this narrative appealed to me, I realized that Disney, and modern society in general, have created a formula for us. They tell us if we have their suggested ingredients, we will be happy.

Everyone wants to be happy. The recipe for happiness is so simple—according to our culture. All we need is an attractive partner who can defeat any villain, a perfect castle, and an endless wardrobe of beautiful clothes. Mix them and presto. We will live happily ever after.

I got to a point where I looked at the recipe for happily ever after and thought, *Okay, I have the ingredients for my fairytale. Now what?*

This is the part of the story Disney leaves out. We work hard to get our happily ever after only to find that pursuing culture's notion of happiness leaves us unfulfilled. We chased after a plan that Disney told us would make us happy, but we forgot to ask God if that was His plan.

I am not saying we won't feel happy if we have an Instagram-worthy family, a perfect house, and a great job. None of those things are inherently bad. But if we put obtaining those things over following God's plan, we won't feel completely fulfilled.

When we watch movies, we tend to place ourselves in the princess' shoes. But what if we aren't called to be Belle? What if God has us written into the story as the candlestick? When we fixate on one narrative and do everything to fit our lives into the princess' plot line, we take away God's ability to write our story.

We can't all be the princess or the prince. If Belle's little village was full of Belles and all their stories were the same, the movie would be weird and confusing. We need to stop forcing ourselves into the princess' role and allow God to write us into His story as whomever He needs us to be.

Instead of viewing ourselves as the main character, we should view Jesus as the main character. Getting Belle and the Beast to fall in love took a team effort. Mrs. Potts had to be a hospitable host for Belle; Lumiere had to give Belle a room and coordinate a fancy dinner for her; and Cogsworth had to be practical and logistical. Every character played a role in achieving the ultimate success of the love story, but none of them was the main character.

If we are called into a big, spotlight role, that's great. But allowing God to put us where He needs us, with Him at the center of the story, means every win for the Kingdom of God is a win for us as supporting characters.

Disney's happily ever after has an expiration date. God's happily ever after is eternal. He needs to direct the movie of our lives, and we need to let Him cast us in a role we had not planned on playing.

In the Word:

> "Many are the plans in the mind of a man, but it is the purpose of the LORD that will stand" (Proverbs 19:21).

> "If then you have been raised with Christ, seek the things that are above, where Christ is, seated at the right hand of God. Set your minds on things that are above, not on things that are on earth. For you have died, and your life is hidden with Christ in God. When Christ who is your life appears, then you also will appear with him in glory" (Colossians 3:1-4).

Reflection Questions:

- In what ways does society promote the narrative that we are meant to be the main character? How can we combat this self-centered idea and place Jesus in the center of our story?
- What gifts do I have that I can use to enhance God's Kingdom? How might my talents and interests be an indication of the path God wants me to pursue?

Chapter Eleven

SPINNING TIRES

When I was in high school, I dated a boy named Matt. He drove a beautiful, black Chevy Silverado. We lived in a nice suburban area with only paved roads—and I don't think he ever had a reason to tow anything—so why he drove a souped-up pickup was beyond me. Nevertheless, I always felt cool riding around in it because it was kind of fancy, and I was seventeen. "He drives a nice car" was still high on the list of qualities I looked for in a boyfriend.

Matt and I lived in southeastern Michigan, but his father lived in the northwestern part of the lower peninsula in a beautiful town called Traverse City. This town was four-and-a-half hours away from where we lived, so during winter break of my senior year of high school, we decided to make a trip up there for a few days and visit.

We drove Matt's cool Silverado. We stayed for four days and explored the area. Winters in northern Michigan are cold and snowy. We spent our time enjoying the winter weather and visiting with Matt's dad. When it was time to go home, we checked the weather, and it looked as if a snowstorm was headed our way. We decided to hit the road earlier than we originally planned in order to beat the weather. The snow had already started falling by the time we left, but I figured Matt could put his truck's four-wheel-drive capabilities to good use and make it through the snow with ease.

An hour into the drive, the weather got worse. "Whiteout" means snow is falling so hard that all around is white. As we drove, the snow fell harder and harder until we could not distinguish looking out the windshield from staring at a giant piece of printer paper. We were in the middle of nowhere, so neither of our cell phones had service.

Matt continued to drive slowly and carefully through the storm. The roads were iced over, so any sudden movements would have caused the truck to slide. We pressed forward until the truck made a loud and unpleasant scraping noise.

"I think we are in a ditch," Matt said in a sheepish, quiet tone.

At first, I did not want to face reality, but I watched as he pressed the gas pedal, and the tires only spun in circles without propelling the truck forward.

I got flashbacks to an episode of *I Shouldn't Be Alive*. A young couple and their baby became lost in a snowstorm. They could not find their way back to civilization and got frostbitten and hungry as they tried for several days to find help. I kept thinking how that was going to be us, and we were going to get stranded in a snowstorm in the middle of nowhere, Michigan.

"Try again," I said.

"It won't work," Matt said.

He pressed the gas, and the tires only spun; we remained in the ditch.

"I'm going to get out and push," I said.

"You can try," he said.

I leaned into the bumper; he pressed the gas; and the tires spun again. But we were still in the ditch. (Hindsight on this: I weighed roughly 110 pounds in high school, and I had noodle arms. I don't know how I thought I was going to push a Silverado out of a ditch.)

"I can't keep trying," Matt said, "because the more I spin the tires, the deeper I dig them into the snow."

"What now?" I asked.

And as we sat in silence—half-frustrated, half-terrified, half trying to decide who would play us in the movie that would eventually be based on our triumphant journey to civilization—we saw a set of yellow headlights headed down the road behind us. The lights got closer and closer, and soon, we saw a truck heading for us through the snow.

Out of the driver's seat walked an older gentleman with a long beard and a red, flannel shirt. I imagined this is what Santa Claus would look like if he went on Weight Watchers and moved to the countryside.

"It looks like you two are stuck!" he said in a rather upbeat and semi-irritating tone.

In my head I thought, *Obviously we're stuck, Country Santa.* But since he was our only hope, I tried not to let my frustration get the better of me and instead chose not to be sassy. The man explained that he was a local in the area. His ministry was to head out in snowstorms with his pick-up and help people who were stuck. My jaw dropped. What a beautiful expression of God's love through service.

He pulled his equipment from the bed of his truck and attached tow lines to the front of Matt's truck. He gave instructions to Matt about when to hit the gas and when to brake. He got into his truck, and he pulled us out of the ditch. He unattached his lines from Matt's truck and prepared to help another snowstorm victim. I grabbed a twenty from my purse—all I had. I handed it to him, but he told me he didn't want my money. He just hoped he could share some of God's love with us and anyone else he helped that day.

As we drove off, neither Matt nor I said anything for a long time. We reflected on the words that man had shared and the way he had sacrificed his afternoon for no purpose other than to share the Gospel with others through service. Since that day, I have thought more about what happened. That situation parallels how our lives feel sometimes.

We can find ourselves in a ditch. Stuck, we experience various emotions. Maybe it's frustration, fear, or looking for someone to blame for our circumstances. What we do know is that we need to get out. But it seems as if every time we try to do it on our own, our tires spin, and we dig ourselves deeper into a hole.

What we might not realize is that trying harder to get out of the circumstance might create a bigger problem. Instead, we need to ask the guy with the towlines and plenty of experience getting people out of ditches to help pull us out. That Guy is Jesus.

Rather than trying harder and spinning our tires, maybe we need to put things in park and wait for help. Jesus wants us to invite Him into the ditch. He wants us to give Him the okay to attach His lines to our stuck vehicle and get us back on the road. And He won't accept our wrinkled money because the price to help us out of the ditch was pre-paid on the cross.

How does your snowy ditch look? Are you stuck in a job you don't feel is your calling? Are you stuck in an unhealthy relationship? Are you living in a sin from which you can't find freedom? Stop spinning your tires and accept God's graciousness and willingness to meet you where you are. Ask Him to grab your life and put you back on the path He has set for you. He wants to meet you there, and the price has been paid. All you must do is admit you can't get out by yourself and invite Him to help you.

In the Word:

> "I sought the Lord, and he answered me and delivered me from all my fears. Those who look to him are radiant, and their faces shall never be ashamed. This poor man cried, and the Lord heard him and saved him out of all his troubles. The angel of the Lord encamps around those who fear him, and delivers them. Oh, taste and see that the Lord is good! Blessed is the man who takes refuge in him" (Psalm 34:4-8).

Reflection Questions:

- What is an area of life you feel stuck in?
- How have you deviated from the path God has intended for you?
- Are you confident asking God to meet you in those difficult places, or do you feel as if you can get out on your own?
- How can your stubbornness prevent you from inviting God into your struggles and fully experiencing His graciousness?

Chapter Twelve

MY MOM

People tell me I look like my mom. I take this as a compliment because my mom is one of the most beautiful women I've ever met. Although I resemble my mom physically, as I have gotten older, I realize we also have similarities in our spiritual journeys. My mom's story is one I admire a lot, and although I could go on about it, I won't.

My mom, much like me, felt called to healthcare. She graduated college as a nurse and spent time working at the University of Michigan. She watched as her early twenties passed, and many of her close college friends—and even her twin sister—fell in love and married. She had dated many quality Christian men, but none of them was a perfect fit. She worked and played bridesmaid in her close friends' weddings and wondered if God was so busy making a husband for everyone else that He forgot to make one for her.

Throughout her twenties, Mom was frustrated at God for not bringing her person into her life. If you are in or have passed your early twenties and are still single, you, too, understand this feeling. We get to a certain age, and we have this desire to find our partner. And if it takes us longer than some of our friends, we think it stinks, watching them fall in love and get married. As happy as we are for them, every wedding we attend is another reminder that we don't have that in our own lives.

My mom continued to wait, work, and pray for her husband, but as the years passed, she remained single and grew more frustrated. Finally, out of frustration and the feeling that God continually answered her prayer with a no, my mom gave up. I love when she tells me this story because her description of her conversation with God that day is classic Mom. She said, "Okay, God, fine. If You want me to be single, I will. It will be You and me, and I'll just have to get over it."

I think we've all been where she was. We've knocked repeatedly on a door that won't open, so we must eventually head in a different direction. But we're human, and we wanted that door to open. When we must walk away from it, we pout. Mom pouted, but because she wanted to live according to God's plan, she stopped knocking on the door of marriage and pursued what she thought was God's call: a life of singleness.

My mom, however, is a tenacious person. She does not like to slow down and always keeps looking ahead to the next thing. Since she was going to be single, she figured she may as well go to graduate school and get her Ph.D. in nursing. (I didn't write this chapter to flex about how cool my mom is, but there's a lot to learn here.)

Mom enrolled at Wayne State University in Detroit. Her mom was a teacher at the time and taught across the hall from a woman whose son was a med student at Wayne as well. Before my mom began classes, her mom and the teacher concocted a plan for the woman's son to give my mom a campus tour.

Mom showed up for the semi-random campus tour, and, of course, the woman's son ended up being the man for whom Mom had prayed. Four months later, they were engaged, and thirty-one years later, they have still maintained the most inspiring marriage I have ever seen. They continue to allow Christ to be the Center of their relationship and the Driving Force of their decisions. They have raised three God-fearing kids, and they continue to choose each other every day as they take on life's challenges.

I tell this story for two reasons. The first is because this story is another beautiful example of why God puts us through difficulties. I am sure, at the time, my mom had no idea why she had to wait so long to meet my dad. I am sure she felt frustrated and confused by the unanswered prayers, closed doors, and lonely feelings as she watched everyone around her get something she wanted but didn't have. But thirty years later, when I was going through the painful breakup that ended my engagement, one of the most comforting things was Mom's story about waiting for her husband.

Weeks after my engagement ended, I wrestled with discomfort and frustration. I wanted to be married; I thought I had found my person; and I continued to battle feelings of loneliness and fear. But it was the story of my mom waiting for my dad, making the desires of her heart known to the Lord and continuing to walk on the path God had set before her, that inspired me to allow God's will in my life.

The amazing thing about God is that all our prayers to Him are precious. If we care about something, so does God. But He loves us enough to wait and answer our prayers at the exact right time. Perhaps, it is to teach us something about waiting, or perhaps He wants to use our experience as a lesson for others.

The second reason concerns my mom's willingness to abide. She put her desire for a relationship aside to follow God's plan. Her obedience led her to meet my dad, but she would not have gotten there had she not let go of her plans.

My mom's story reminds me of the story of Abraham and Isaac in Genesis 22. Abraham and his wife Sarah wanted to have a child, but they were too old. Sarah was ninety, and Abraham was one hundred. Biologically, the having-kids ship had sailed. But they faithfully prayed, and God gave them a son whom they named Isaac. God, however, wanted to know Abraham would obey Him, so He instructed Abraham to take Isaac to the top of a mountain and sacrifice him.

Abraham loved his son and had waited so long to have him, but he wanted to obey God. He did what God asked and took his son to the top of the mountain, built an altar, and put him on it. As he held a knife over Isaac's body, an angel appeared and told him to stop. God was pleased with Abraham because Abraham prioritized obedience to God over his love for his son for whom he had waited so long. God promised to bless Abraham's family for generations to come.

I'm sorry, but is no one else stunned by that story? Abraham loved God so much that he was willing to *sacrifice* his *only child* to obey Him. That is insane, but God wanted to see that Abraham loved him more than anything else in the world.

Mom loved and trusted God. She prioritized her obedience to God above the desires of her heart, letting go of that desire to obey God's plan. Because of her obedience, God opened the door for her to meet my dad.

I think about this a lot and try to find ways to apply it to my life. Are there things I desire so much that I choose to pursue them instead of God? Do I cling to these things so tightly that I would hold onto them even if God asked me to give them up? Is my obedience to God and my trust in His plan so strong that I will allow it to guide my life?

We can feel as if God isn't answering our prayers when He isn't saying no or being silent. But oftentimes, He is only saying not now. Unlike the plans we can create for ourselves, God's timing is perfect. None of the people He places in our life show up tardy because they were caught in traffic. None of the experiences He asks us to walk through happen a few years before we're ready for them.

It can be uncomfortable when we desire something to happen immediately, and it doesn't happen even after we pray about it. A key part of trusting in God's plan is believing His timing works out just the way it needs to. We need to obey and trust Him with the desires of our hearts and pray for His will to be done through every one of them.

My mom is an example of complete obedience and trust in God's plan. It's not easy, and at times, it can be confusing; but allowing God's will to be done, despite the unknown, brings blessings and allows us to live a better life than the one we had planned.

In the Word:

> "Therefore do not be anxious, saying, 'What shall we eat?' or 'What shall we drink?' or 'What shall we wear?' For the Gentiles seek after all these things, and your Heavenly

Father knows that you need them all. But seek first the kingdom of God and his righteousness, and all these things will be added to you" (Matthew 6:31-33).

"Delight yourself in the LORD, and he will give you the desires of your heart. Commit your way to the Lord; trust in him, and he will act" (Psalms 37:4-5).

Reflection Questions:

- Think of a time you wanted something that didn't come to you immediately. How did that feel?
- How does our culture's expectation of instant gratification influence your ability to wait on God and His timing?
- Have you ever placed your pursuit of an earthly desire (relationships, family, career, etc.) over your pursuit of Jesus? How can you ensure your priorities are always God first and everything else second?

Chapter Thirteen

CANNONBALLS

Psychology has always fascinated me. I took several psychology courses in my undergraduate education. The mind is a fascinating thing, and there is so much we still don't know about it. All areas of the field interest me, but I am particularly interested in learned behaviors. Except for a few instinctual reactions, most of our behavior is shaped by the things we have learned, either through modeling or conditioning. What amazes me is that we learn a behavior much quicker through conditioning if our associated experience with a particular stimulus is negative or painful.

I adopted my dog when he was two years old. He already knew a lot of things when I got him, but there were a lot of behaviors I wanted him to know that he had not yet learned. For instance, he knew how to sit when I told him, but teaching him to roll over took a few days of teaching and a lot of reward treats. He is much better at it now, but teaching him to roll over was a long process. That behavior had to be conditioned with a positive stimulus. I said a command; he rolled over; and he got a treat. After doing that several times, he rolled over at my command without a treat because he associated the command with something good.

We have a big backyard, and we put up an electric fence for him. Doing this entails showing the dog where the boundaries of the yard are. He wears a collar that beeps as he approaches the fence line, forewarning him that if he goes any farther, he may get shocked. It took only one instance of him going too close to the fence line and getting shocked for him to learn not to leave the yard. Now, even the sound of the warning beep sends him running toward the house.

Think about that for a minute. Learning a behavior like rolling over takes a few days and a lot of bribery with treats. But when the behavior was associated with a bad experience—getting shocked to teach him to stay in the yard—a single, painful experience was enough for him never to leave the yard again.

I think about that a lot when I talk to people who are afraid to trust God's plan. I often hear people relate their experience with Jesus back to a painful memory and claim that is why they have a hard time trusting Him. Things such as "I trusted God, and then my family member became ill," or "I trusted God, and then I lost my job."

I get it. We are shocked. Now, every time we think of letting God have control of our life, we associate it with the pain of that experience, and we fear letting it happen again. That's psychology at play. We learn much quicker to avoid a painful thing than we do to trust a good thing. The unfortunate reality is that one shock is often all it takes to make us walk away from the Lord.

The ability to trust God with our lives does not always come naturally when we think about how our brains are wired. One perceived bad experience, and our minds lead us to think God doesn't have our backs. We need to reshape the way we view God's plan.

God doesn't promise we won't get shocked, so we can't immediately associate a bad or painful experience with God being untrustworthy. We talked a lot in previous chapters about why God might ask us to go through trials. Although they are difficult to endure, He asks us to walk through these things because He loves us and wants us to continue to learn and grow in Him. He might be showing us we are too close to crossing an unsafe boundary.

When I was a child, we vacationed in Florida. The place where we stayed had a pool, and my dad and I played in it for hours. I was too young to swim at the time, but my dad held me and kept me afloat. We also played in the pool with my brothers, splashing each other and jumping off the deck into the pool where dad waited to catch us. I don't recall this experience, but I have heard the story several times.

I was a fearless kid. I jumped into many new experiences with little calculation or regard for my safety. The pool was another one of those things that did not scare me. I jumped off the edge with little thought that I did not know how to swim. Experience had taught me that my dad would catch me and ensure I was safe.

One time, however, I made my way to the pool by myself and jumped in. Since I couldn't swim because I was a toddler, I sank to the bottom. Dad looked for me and walked to the edge of the pool and peered in. He saw me standing on the bottom of the pool, completely submerged. I was not afraid or distressed but just looked up at him through the water. Dad naturally rushed to pull me out of the water to safety. I'm sure his heart had sunk in that moment.

I had learned to jump in with no regard. I was conditioned to believe I could dive in, despite not knowing how to swim, and my dad would keep me afloat. My mistake that time was jumping in without confirming my dad was there to catch me.

It takes us longer to learn something when we associate it with a positive reward. Just like my dog learning to roll over, our brains are wired to proceed with caution. If we do something enough times and see a positive outcome, we know it is reliable, and we will be more comfortable repeating that behavior.

But we must ignore this test-the-waters-before-jumping-in mentality when we put our faith in God. He asks us to understand that the difficult times we have endured were for our benefit and that every blessing comes from Him. When we view our lives through this lens, trusting God's plan is much easier.

As followers of Christ, we are asked to imitate the toddler jumping into the pool, despite having no idea how to swim. When we make sure our Heavenly Father is present, we won't have to worry about Him letting us drown. But when we forget to make sure Jesus is present and we jump in anyway, we will end up like me that day at the pool and sink to the bottom.

Faith requires trusting that God will catch us, even though it seems as if we are leaping into a dangerous situation. We know the nature of God and that His promise to provide for us is good. Just as my dad would have never let me drown, God will always catch us when we leap into the places He has called us to go. When we jump without first ensuring that we are in God's presence, we are more likely to end up in a bad situation.

How unfortunate if we never jumped off the edge of the pool at all. If we believed the lie that God's ways are not the best and instead chose never to leap. We can miss out on the incredible things God has in store. We might even fail to fulfill a role God needs us to fill for His Kingdom.

I love the story of Peter walking on water in Matthew 14 because it applies to this complete and fearless trust in God's power. Jesus and the disciples were on a boat on the Sea of Galilee. Just before this, Jesus had fed five thousand plus people with only five loaves of bread and two fish.

Before dawn, Jesus had wanted alone time to pray. He left the disciples on the boat. When He finished praying, He walked on water to get back to the boat. The disciples saw Him and feared Him. They thought He was a ghost. But Peter reacted differently. Often in the Bible, Peter was this big, bold character with child-like faith. Again here, Peter was daring. He said to Jesus, "Okay, if it's You . . . call me over to You on the water."

Can you imagine? The logistical side of me cringes at this. Had it been me, I would have probably said, "Jesus, if it's You, come back in the boat, and let's get You a cup of coffee since it's, like, five a.m." Peter had this faith in Jesus that is beyond the scope of human rationality. Peter stepped onto the water. But as soon as Peter got scared and lost faith, he sank. Jesus asked Peter why he doubted Him and lost faith.

What can we learn from Peter? For me, the takeaway is always to step into the places where God has called us and to keep trusting Him when that place becomes scary or difficult. This is a theme to which we keep returning. Sometimes, we can't see the bigger picture, but if we live faithfully, we can know we are going to be okay. But better than okay. We will be living according to God's plan.

When we jump into unfamiliar places—but make sure Jesus is in the water to catch us—we will learn quickly that He will not let us drown. A little jump into His arms will show us He has our back. Once we are conditioned to know He will keep us afloat, we will get more comfortable cannonballing into those unfamiliar and scary places since we know it is His will for us.

In the Word:

> "Therefore, since we are surrounded by so great a cloud of witnesses, let us also lay aside every weight, and sin which clings so closely, and let us run with endurance the race that is set before us" (Hebrews 12:1).

Reflection Questions:

- Has God ever called you to cannonball into a situation that seems unfamiliar or scary?
- How can you respond to God when He asks you to blindly trust Him and step into something you hadn't planned?
- Do you trust God enough to obey whatever He might ask you to do? How can you strengthen that trust and continue to obey His call on your life?

Chapter Fourteen

THE CHASE

Something I have heard many times in my Christian life is that we should constantly chase after Jesus. The premise is that we should make it our mission to pursue a relationship with our Heavenly Father. I think it's a good message, but I have never been fond of the concept of chasing God.

In college, I competed in triathlon racing. During most races, the runner settles with a group of athletes who run at about the same pace. The runner has race buddies who run about neck and neck the whole race, but then some are maybe fifty yards ahead. I am a competitor at heart, and I always focus on the runners ahead of me. I push myself and dig deep to catch up to them. Regardless of whether I beat them in the end, I relentlessly chase those ahead of me.

When I think about chasing God, I visualize Him as the competitor ahead of me. In a lot of ways, this makes my relationship with Jesus feel unattainable. Chasing after Jesus implies that I am pushing myself as hard as I can to catch up to Him while He is running far ahead of me. But I don't think that's how a relationship with Christ should feel.

What if we rephrased that popular Christian phrase "chase after Jesus" to say "run alongside Jesus"?

When I was in college, my best friend and roommate was notorious for walking incredibly fast. I remember the first day of classes in our freshman year. We planned to walk together to the main academic building on campus. I thought she was trying to get rid of me because she zoomed by all the other students on her way to Alter Hall.

After a few days of living with her, I realized fast was just her pace. Within a few weeks of walking to classes together, I found keeping up with her wasn't as difficult as it was on the first day of classes. By my senior year, I was comfortable walking at her pace wherever we went.

Instead of chasing after Jesus, what if we practiced walking *with* Him? Much like chasing after God, walking at His pace takes practice and discipline. It isn't always easy to keep in step with Him, and moving at His pace might take getting used to. But soon, the pace He has set for us will feel comfortable.

How does it look to practice Jesus' pace? This is something I have had to work hard at in my life. First, it involves making it a priority to spend time with Him every day in prayer and devotion. That time is a lot like the pre-race chat I have with my coaches before I compete in a triathlon. I can hear from Jesus what the strategy is and how He thinks I should approach the day.

Walking with Jesus also requires understanding He oversees our speed. Often, I find myself frustrated that I haven't reached the next thing in my life—whether a relationship, a job opportunity, or a milestone. Instead of waiting for His timing so we can arrive at the next thing together, I run ahead of Jesus and get there on my own. In reality, His pace doesn't have me getting to that point yet. Every time I try to outrun God, I am reminded why His timing is much better than mine. I am never equipped to face the next thing alone, so keeping in step with Jesus is vital.

Practicing my roommate's famous speed walk to class took some getting accustomed to, but once I was comfortable with her pace, keeping up with her was second nature. With some discipline and trust in God's perfect timing, we will experience how fulfilling a life is when we walk with Jesus. He isn't trying to outrun us in an exhausting chase. Rather, He desires our company to walk together through life.

In the Word:

> "Lead me in your truth and teach me, for you are the God of my salvation; for you I wait all the day long. Remember your mercy, O Lord, and your steadfast love, for they have been from of old. Remember not the sins of my youth or my transgressions; according to your steadfast love remember me, for the sake of your goodness, O Lord! Good and upright is the Lord; therefore he instructs sinners in the way. He leads the humble in what is right, and teaches the humble his way" (Psalm 25:5-9).

Reflection Questions:

- Have you had times when following God felt more like a tiring chase than a comfortable walk?
- What are ways you can practice the pace of Jesus and be comfortable with the timing He has for your life?

Chapter Fifteen

INFLUENCE

Some say we are a compilation of the five people with whom we are the closest. I have no idea if that is accurate or is based on research, but it might be. Even if the number may not be accurate, I think the idea holds true. Who we surround ourselves with shapes who we are and the direction in which we head.

This relates to the idea of following God's plan because it's more difficult to go where we are called if the people we are with are not headed in the same direction. We need to find people who encourage us and cheer us on as we step into the things that God has called us to do.

The enemy speaks through other people to lure us away from God's plan. For me, this has been as simple as someone making a discouraging comment about something God has called me to do, and then I begin doubting if I am doing the right thing.

Instead, we should surround ourselves with people who encourage us to follow our purpose and celebrate our wins. A godly, supportive community can be one of the best ways to ensure we are on God's intended path.

I think about this idea in the same way I think about river currents. The odds are that a leaf in a river will float in the same direction as the current. It may get stuck on a rock or a log occasionally, but most of the time, it travels in the same direction as the water flows.

The people we surround ourselves with act a lot like the current. Their attitudes and values have the power to carry us in the same direction that the Lord wants us to head. But the opposite can happen when we surround ourselves with people who don't have our best interests at heart.

I've seen this in my own life. Surrounding myself with people whose currents flowed in the opposite direction of the one God wanted me to head sucked me in their direction rather than God's. Before I realized it, I had deviated from God's plan because I did not choose my friends carefully. It isn't always apparent that the people we surround ourselves with are leading us astray. The enemy is sneakier than that.

I remember when I first realized the thoughts I had written might bring peace to other people struggling with the same things I had wrestled. I prayed about it, and God placed it in my heart to turn them into a book. Stepping into that calling confused me. I thought I was too young, unknowledgeable, and unworthy to fulfill that role. Fear caused me to remain silent about my work for many months.

I finally talked about this call to write with some friends. Their reactions revealed the direction of their current versus the direction of mine. Some people whom I viewed as close to me were not always rooting for me to pursue God's call.

Some people said nothing or rolled their eyes as I shared this new chapter (pun intended) of my life as a writer. I heard comments such as, "What do you even have to write about?" or "How do you know your writing is going to be theologically sound?" Someone close to me asked, "Aren't you afraid you're going to misuse God's Word and cause more harm than good?"

Soon, I began doubting the Lord's task, which was to share my faith experiences with others through a book. I questioned if I were too young or untalented. I wondered if anyone would even be interested in my life experiences. And I feared I would misuse God's Word in my writing.

After much prayer and reflection, I realized I was capable. The enemy, however, had used people whom I thought were close to me to pull me into their current with their comments. On the other hand, those individuals who supported and encouraged me were those whose currents flowed toward the Kingdom. They drove me in the direction I needed to go.

But why talk about community and relationships when, up until this point, we have only discussed God's plan when it challenges us? The people we hold the closest can pull us away from God's plan. They can discourage us from stepping into the places we are called and instead into those places that deviate from God's path.

A great example comes from Matthew 26. Jesus is on trial, and Peter denies he ever knew Jesus. Earlier in the New Testament, Peter did some amazing things as a disciple. He had a bold faith and walked with God, stepping into the places where the Lord called him. But when following Jesus grew challenging, Peter found himself among a crowd of high priests and other people who hated Jesus and His mission on earth.

As soon as Peter found himself among people whose current flowed in the opposite direction, he got pulled in. They asked Peter if he was with Jesus of Galilee and if he knew Who Jesus was. Three times, Peter said he had no idea Who Jesus was.

Peter's experience shows how easy it is to get pulled into the current of those headed away from God. Even after years of serving God's kingdom, Peter opposed Jesus after only a few moments with a bad crowd. The enemy uses the influence of those around us to pry us away from God, just as he did with Peter.

Satan is deceptive. He can lead us astray through those around us without us even realizing we're being rerouted. We need to surround ourselves with people who will encourage us and cheer us on as we enter the places God calls. Identify those people who will always want to see you fulfill God's purpose for your life. At the end of the day, a win for the Kingdom of God is a win for them. These are the people who will help us stick to God's plan and make our journey worth the while.

In the Word:

> "And let us consider how to stir up one another to love and good works, not neglecting to meet together, as is the habit of some, but encouraging one another, and all the more as you see the Day drawing near" (Hebrews 10:24-25).

Reflection Questions:

- Who are the five people you consider closest to you? Would you be happy with whom you are if you were a composite of their personalities?

- Do the people you surround yourself with support you? Do they celebrate your wins and encourage you through your losses?
- How has community influenced your behaviors either for the better or the worse?
- How can you seek community that will keep you on the path God has set for you?

Chapter Sixteen

PURPOSE ANXIETY

The term "purpose anxiety" has surfaced in social sciences and popular culture within the last few years. We discussed it in some of my undergraduate psychology courses, and I have heard it pop up a few times on campus in discussions about mental health or selecting a career path. But even more than that, I have watched this so-called philosophy manifest itself in many of my friends and peers in their early twenties.

Essentially, purpose anxiety refers to deep-rooted distress caused by the age-old question, "What is the purpose of my life?" This unsettlement with people's life calling has been on the rise in recent decades, and secular psychologists have studied ways to combat this distress from permeating our lives.

I watched this fear cripple many of my school friends. I lived in a big house in college with several roommates. Each of us had different majors and different life ambitions, but one of the girls became consumed by purpose anxiety. There were nights we tried to console her as she lay in a fetal position and sobbed, wailing about how she didn't like her major, didn't know what she wanted to do with her life, and didn't know what life was about.

As a Christian, I have always known the purpose of my life was much bigger than me. But she did not know Who the Lord is, and the enemy

97

used that to confuse her and lead her to question the meaning of life. I couldn't relate to the feelings she had, but as I had deeper conversations with other people our age, I realized this issue was pervasive in our culture, especially with young adults and young professionals.

A lot of the people I went to school with knew what it was like to curl up in a ball in their bed and cry while they questioned their future and their purpose. Something that interests me, however, is that as our culture deviates further from God, purpose anxiety becomes more prominent. When we forget about Who God is, we forget about who we are.

I don't think this is coincidental. As our culture drives a larger wedge between ourselves and the Lord, we lose a sense of our purpose. The Lord is the One Who gives our lives purpose.

Having a relationship with the Lord and remaining faithful to Him alleviates any anxiety we might feel about our purpose. If we want to know what we were created for, we need to draw near to our Creator.

Only through Jesus can we understand why God placed us here. We are designed to be the hands and feet of God's Kingdom and are equipped with unique talents and abilities to go into our communities and use those gifts to share Who God is. Our purpose is to be faithful to God and use everything He has given to us to make more disciples.

That doesn't seem all that complicated. So, if it's that simple, why does our culture suffer from so much distress over the meaning of life? Because we are answering the question from a worldly perspective. We are looking to secular psychologists, mental health resources, and popular science to tell us why we were created. If we view the same question from a biblical perspective, the answer is much simpler.

To illustrate this, I want to reference an article from *HealthLine. com* called, "What Is 'Purpose Anxiety' and Do You Have It?" The article defines purpose anxiety as "the anxiety we feel when we don't have a sense of purpose but are all too aware that it's missing."[1] It suggests five signs to look for which may indicate we struggle with purpose anxiety: frequent switching between jobs or companies, feelings of failure or inadequacy, negative comparison to others, fear of never discovering our true purpose, and the inability to recognize our accomplishments.

But what's the solution? The article suggests our purpose comes from self-knowledge. Since we can't look outwardly for our purpose, we need to look inwardly. Still confused? Yeah, me too. "Authentic purpose comes from knowing yourself," the author says.[2] That's the problem. Our generation is increasingly depressed and anxious because we don't know ourselves well enough. I think we know ourselves today just as well as those in the generations before us, so to me, that doesn't feel like an accurate assessment of the issue.

But the article gives more tips, such as the need to create our own purpose, not find it. We can't view purpose as something to be discovered. Rather we should go out and actively seek it. Maybe this argument isn't all bad, but we don't have to hunt down our purpose because God has already given us one.

And the third thing, according to the article, we should do is constantly shape our purpose through life experiences. We should let life happen to us and use what we experience to point us in the

---

1   Elaine Mead, "What Is 'Purpose Anxiety' and Do You Have It?," HealthLine. com, June 1, 2020, https://www.healthline.com/health/what-is-purpose-anxiety-do-you-have-it.
2   Ibid.

direction of our purpose. This point seems to contradict the second tip to combat purpose anxiety.

That this article contradicts itself reveals that answers to this question, which aren't based on God's Word, can't solve our problem. Society realizes a pervasive distress associated with what we were created for but can't generate a real solution to the issue.

The article took me about ten minutes to read and left me utterly confused. But I am not trying to downgrade the article. I realize the author applies the skewed and confused ideas of the world to a deep, theological question. The article does the best it can at using the secular ideology of self-promotion and gratification to solve an innately spiritual problem.

The central arguments in this article are the exact reasons society keeps missing the mark, and anxiety about the meaning of life runs rampant. We look inward and use our selfish ambition to glorify ourselves to discover our purpose. We make our plans based on what will benefit us and bring the world's attention.

When we shift our focus to God, our anxiety diminishes. Doing so is a simple yet effective way to combat purpose anxiety. Instead of looking inward and getting to know ourselves better, as the article suggests, we should look to Heaven and get to know our Creator better. Instead of asking how we can bring fame and glory to ourselves, we can ask how we can bring fame and glory to the name of Jesus.

Once we recognize we already have a purpose, pursuing it is much less self-seeking than our culture thinks, and our lives change. Suddenly, we aren't living for ourselves, but we're living for others— and most importantly, for Christ. We don't have to find purpose from deep introspection or chase goals that won't fulfill us.

We can ditch the planners, the Google calendar, and the anxiety we feel when we wonder what we are supposed to do with our lives. All we must do is say yes to the plans God already has for us. We can wake up every day and pursue Him. We can follow Him into the valley; listen to Him when He calls us somewhere we don't want to go; and use our talents, abilities, and passions to glorify Him. When we surrender our plans and let God control our agenda, we won't stress over what is around the corner.

Suppose an architect was building a house, and he decided to put a support beam through the living room. If we took the support beam outside and looked at it, we would think it was a useless piece of wood. But if we put the support beam in the house, its purpose would be evident. Isolating something and considering its purpose without the whole picture for context is confusing.

The *Healthline* article takes us by ourselves away from our Creator and asks us to consider what we are good for. Away from God and His purpose for us, we are like a support beam disconnected from its purpose. Purpose and plans become much clearer when we look away from ourselves and to God. We need to note where He has placed us and understand our purpose is much bigger than ourselves.

The article ends with this quote: "I'm slowly learning that my sense of purpose in life is truly in my own hands."[3] We only let ourselves down if we think we create purpose for our lives. Take it from me, I have tried to create purpose for myself. But the moment I turned to God and surrendered my plans to Him—making my life's purpose to glorify Him—my anxiety about the future faded.

---

3   Ibid.

When isolated from our Creator, we will never understand our purpose. Ask God why He placed you where you are right now, and then ask Him how He wants to use you. Your purpose is to complete the mission God has created uniquely for you.

In the Word:

> "Only let each person lead the life that the Lord has assigned to him, and to which God has called him. This is my rule in all the churches" (1 Corinthians 7:17).

> "And Jesus came and said to them, 'All authority in heaven and on earth has been given to me. Go therefore and make disciples of all nations, baptizing them in the name of the Father and of the Son and of the Holy Spirit, teaching them to observe all that I have commanded you. And behold, I am with you always, to the end of the age'" (Matthew 28:18-20).

Reflection Questions:

- Do you struggle with purpose anxiety? Do you know what you were created to do?

- How can you say yes to the plans the Lord has for you and step into the purpose to which He has called you?

- What are some practical ways you can replace the lie that your plans are the best plans with the truth that the Lord's plans are best? Ask the Lord to make clear His plans for you and be willing to go where He calls you.

Chapter Seventeen

LICENSE PLATE

When we were kids, we had a small camper we pulled behind our old pick-up truck. We took it to different cities for family vacations. I am so thankful for that time. We made some of our fondest family memories during our camping years.

That was a different time, so what I will relate would not fly now. The truck was not spacious. We had to open the driver's door to open the back door. The back seats were quite small, and the doors opened toward each other. The road trips were long, and our room was limited. I was the youngest child, the only girl, and tiny. On our way to our destination, one of my brothers would lie on the floor; one would stretch across the seats; and I would lie in a hammock that my parents strung between the garment hooks.

This setup was the best because everyone got more room, and I thought riding in a hammock was the coolest thing ever. No chance that such a setup would be acceptable today.

No road trip is complete without good car games. We often played the "What Does That Cloud Look Like" game. That game was never the same after my middle brother looked at a cloud and said, "That one looks like a crab chasing its destiny." To this day, I have no clue what that means, but it gave us all a good laugh.

A couple of other favorites were I Spy and The License Plate Game. For the license plate game, we looked at the license plates of the cars on the road and tried to find one from each of the fifty states. It would usually take a few road trips to find them all, and my mom was responsible for keeping a list of the states we had seen and those we still needed to find. Nothing satisfied us more than spotting one of the obscure license plates like Hawaii—one we don't normally see while driving through a cornfield in Ohio.

The license plate game was fun because we wondered where the people came from, how they got to where they were, and where they were headed. We used their license plates to identify and draw conclusions about them.

I once listened to a podcast about not identifying ourselves by our past but by our position as forgiven children of God. I liked the message, but it didn't sit well with me. I love the idea of not defining ourselves by our past, but even on the path God has set for us, we will always have the license plate that identifies from where we have come.

This once hit me hard. A friend of mine sent me a screenshot of a post made by my ex-fiancé and his new girlfriend—the same one with whom he had cheated on me. The posts had been made months after he and I called off our engagement. As I looked at the photos, I broke down and cried.

I hadn't cried in months about what had happened. I didn't miss him, nor did I wish I was the girl with him in the photos. I had worked through that trauma in the face of the Lord, and I thought I had healed and moved on. But my emotional reaction upset me. I didn't want to be defined by my past hurt. Rather, I wanted to be defined by the growth I had accomplished despite that hurt.

After thinking and praying about this episode, I realized I would carry the hurt for the rest of my life. If I forget the pain of that experience and don't include it as a part of my story, I will turn my back on the reason God asked me to walk through that trial.

I don't want to walk into a room and immediately be seen as the girl whose engagement ended in gut-wrenching infidelity, but I cannot pretend my experience was not a part of my journey with God. My license plate will always have that experience written on it, but it doesn't change my direction. That direction is wherever the Lord leads.

In my experience with the Christian community, as it relates to trauma and hurt, I have often been advised to work through the trauma with the Lord and then pretend the hurt didn't happen. Of course, no one phrases it like that, but the underlying message always felt as if I should replace my past hurt with the Lord's hope and move on.

That message troubles me. I think it's still wise to discuss the trials we have experienced as a testament to God's goodness in bringing us through those difficult times. These things are our license plates, an indication of where we have come from, but they do not influence the path we are on.

Someone whom I think has displayed this beautifully is my brother, Ryan. His walk with the Lord has been anything but smooth. He struggled with certain sins and illnesses that drove a wedge between him and God. But through invasive heart surgery, both his physical and spiritual heart were made new. Today, Ryan is a spiritual role model to me and many others. He never denies his not-so-perfect past or sweeps under the rug those years he spent away from God.

Ryan is an example of wearing a license plate—but not as an indicator of who he is but of what God has done through him. Our plates provide symbols of where we are headed, regardless of those hardships. God calls us to use the lessons from the trials we have experienced to shed light on the many ways He works through us to redeem our stories. The ability to walk according to God's plan is independent of the things written on our license plates.

What we have done or gone through doesn't diminish God's ability to write us into His plan, but that does not mean we should deny our past experiences. The apostle Paul is an incredible example of this. Paul was formerly named Saul and was responsible for executing many first-century Christians. After Jesus transformed him, Paul was eventually sent to prison for proclaiming Jesus's name. Behind bars, Paul wrote letters that became some of the most influential pieces of the New Testament. Many think Paul is one of the most important figures in Christian history.

Paul didn't hide his past. Prisoner and murder were written on his license plate and will forever be a part of his story, but it did not change his ability to head in the right direction. Despite what his license plate said, Paul stepped into the place to which the Lord had called him. Through the things he did in his lifetime, he changed the hearts of people for generations to come.

As we close, I want us to look back at some of the things we have discussed. We talked about the reason we endure trials and the ways we can prepare our hearts and minds to endure inevitable trials in a godly way. We looked at godly community and council, as well as our need to follow our passions and use our talents to pursue God's plan.

And we discussed letting go of the anxiety and fear we have over the future and how we can be comfortable allowing God to call the shots and dictate our path.

Where we have come from and where God wants to take us are two separate things. Mistakes we have made, sins we have lived in, hardships we have endured, or times we have chosen to walk out of step with the Lord do not exclude us from receiving God's love, nor do they change God's plan. He desires our heart, and He longs for our trust.

Allow God to lead you into those unfamiliar places. Lean on Him when he walks you through valleys and trials. Never assume He does not have a plan for your life just because your license plate says you are coming from an imperfect place. Instead, use those experiences to show the world you are following a path that was set forth for you by a sovereign and almighty God.

In the Word:

> "Therefore, if anyone is in Christ, he is a new creation. The old has passed away; behold, the new has come. All this is from God, who through Christ reconciled us to himself and gave us the ministry of reconciliation; that is, in Christ God was reconciling the world to himself, not counting their trespasses against them, and entrusting to us the message of reconciliation. Therefore, we are ambassadors for Christ, God making his appeal through

us. We implore you on behalf of Christ, be reconciled to
God. For our sake he made him to be sin who knew no sin,
so that in him we might become the righteousness of God"
(2 Corinthians 5:17-21).

Reflection Questions:

- What are past experiences or trials you have gone through
  that you wish may never have happened or that you try
  to hide from your story?

- Why might it be important that you acknowledge and
  bring to light these hardships?

- How can you include your past as part of your story while
  still ensuring that "follower of Jesus" is your primary
  identity?

ACKNOWLEDGMENTS

People have credited me for writing this book. Truthfully, I have written nothing on these pages that didn't result from the influence of the incredible people who have supported me throughout my journey.

To my parents, Steven and Molly, thank you for showing me what it looks like to take up my cross daily and follow the Lord. Thank you for pushing me to be more like Him every day. Thank you for your constant love and support, for the tears of mine that you have dried, and for the comfort you have provided in some of my darkest moments. I would not be me without you, and I am forever grateful to have you both as parents, counselors, and role models.

To my brothers, Bryce and Ryan—each of you has shaped my life in ways you could never understand. Bryce, thank you for the way you have led by example. I am daily in awe of your discipline and devotion to the Lord. Watching as you have led your beautiful family and loved those around you with the love of Christ inspires me daily. Your wisdom has guided me through some of my most difficult trials, and I am forever grateful. Ryan, thank you for being my best friend. I am so thankful to have you as someone on whom I can always rely. Your goofy side always makes me smile, but you also provide wise words and godly counsel that have been vital to my spiritual growth.

To my sisters-in-love, Jenna and Kortney. Jenna, thank you for the energy and spirit you have brought to our family. You impress me every day with the way you have both wisdom and love for Jesus. Your fun-loving spirit brightens every room you enter. Kortney, in the short amount of time you have been in our family, you have transformed from a stranger to a sister and a best friend. The way you see God's hand in every situation and have provided guidance when I need it most has been integral to my spiritual growth. I am forever grateful to you both. I am thankful my brothers married two of the most beautiful, godly women I have ever known. I am blessed beyond measure to have you both as role models, prayer partners, and friends.

To my grandmother, Joan, I am blessed to have you to look up to. You handle yourself with the grace and dignity that I aspire to achieve. Thank you for supporting me in everything and for showing up at every choir concert, dance recital, and horse show. Thank you for showing me what it means to love those around you with the love of Christ and for extending to me unconditional love as well. Your example has shown me what it means to be a Proverbs 31 woman, and your guidance has made me who I am today.

To my remaining grandparents, Alan, Gray and Kay. Whether you are on Earth or with Jesus, thank you for your influence on my life. Your combined love and support have made me feel blessed beyond all measure.

To my dearest college friends, Abby and Cassandra. Girls, we have been through so much together. Thank you both for showing me unconditional love when I needed it most. Thank you for the laughs we have shared, the tears we have shed, and the light you have each shone on me. Your impact on my life has taught me so much, and your friendship is something I will forever cherish.

To my dear friend and roommate, Lily. Lil, you are one of the most awe-inspiring people I have ever met. You have demonstrated how it looks to walk out your faith, even when choosing the path of the Lord has felt lonely and difficult. Your ability to listen and surrender to the will of God is incredible and something I look up to. You have modeled how it looks to follow Jesus in a generation where it is difficult. You have shown me love and support, and I am forever grateful for our friendship and your influence.

To my cousin, Lincoln. Thank you for coming alongside of me during one of my most difficult times in life and sharing with me in my grief and heartache. You are one of the few people I knew genuinely understood what I was feeling and you encourages me to continue to seek the Lord's guidance and turn to Him for comfort.

To my small group girls from Woodside Bible Church—each of you has been an answered prayer. You have provided me with challenging spiritual community and dear friendships I have come to cherish. Thank you for your support and love and for the way you have spurred me on in my walk with the Lord.

To Ambassador International, thank you for helping me share my story. Thank you for your commitment to spreading the truth in a world that needs God's message. I appreciate the hard work you do with all your authors.

To my friends and family not yet mentioned. While I wish I could name each of you and thank you for the role you played in my life and spiritual journey, know that your influence has not gone unappreciated. I thank God daily for the people He has put in my life. Each of you means a great deal to me, and I would not be who I am without your love and guidance.

To you, my reader, thank you for accompanying me on this journey and allowing me to share parts of my life with you. I hope you have grown from reading my words just as I have grown from writing them. I prayed for you as I wrote this book, and I continue to pray for you. I have confidence that no matter where you are on your faith journey, you have the potential to be a champion for the Kingdom of God. I would love to hear parts of your story.

BIBLIOGRAPHY

Keller, W. Phillip. *A Shepherd Looks at Psalm 23*. Grand Rapids: Zondervan, 2018.

Mead, Elaine. "What Is 'Purpose Anxiety' and Do You Have It?" *Healthline.com*, June 1, 2020, https://www.healthline.com/health/what-is-purpose-anxiety-do-you-have-it.

ABOUT THE AUTHOR

Bailey Lynn was born outside of Detroit, Michigan. She has been passionate about writing since she was a little girl, although her stories then included more dragons and princesses than the stories she writes now. Bailey graduated from Xavier University in Cincinnati, Ohio, with a Bachelor of Science in Biology and is currently pursuing a graduate education to become a physician assistant at the University of Detroit Mercy. In her time away from studying, Bailey enjoys baking, training for and competing in triathlons (to burn off the calories she gained eating her baked goods), and cuddling her rescued beagle, Beau. *Unforeseen* is Bailey's first book. She can be contacted at baileylynnbooks.com, baileylynnbooks@gmail.com, or @baileylmc.

Ambassador International's mission is to magnify the Lord Jesus Christ and promote His Gospel through the written word.

We believe through the publication of Christian literature, Jesus Christ and His Word will be exalted, believers will be strengthened in their walk with Him, and the lost will be directed to Jesus Christ as the only way of salvation.

For more information about
AMBASSADOR INTERNATIONAL
please visit:

www.ambassador-international.com
@AmbassadorIntl
www.facebook.com/AmbassadorIntl

Thank you for reading this book!

You make it possible for us to fulfill our mission, and we are grateful for your partnership.

To help further our mission, please consider leaving us a review on your social media, favorite retailer's website, Goodreads or Bookbub, or our website.

More from Ambassador International

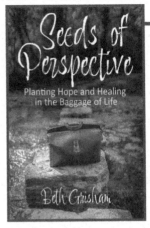

In *Seeds of Perspective*, women of all ages and walks of life willingly poured out their most difficult life situations as a personal sacrifice to help others process and find hope and healing in their own worst mistakes. They believe that remembering and sharing their stories awakens in each of us a deeper understanding of God's promise to redeem our lives for His glory and His purposes and to bring beauty from the ashes of our past.

Finding Hope and Strength in God is a twelve-month devotional with different themes for each month focused on pointing you to your all-sufficient Savior, Who will give you strength and hope to face the day and to live a meaningful and fulfilling Christian life. Its practical approach to life will help you navigate real-life situations with tangible solutions to help you find meaning, hope, strength, and courage despite the tumultuous eventualities of life.

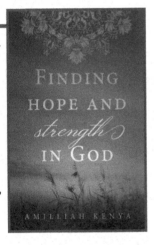

The Ministry of the Unveiled Face grounds us in the simplicity of sharing Christ in the everyday. The meekness of the call lies in our being responsive and obedient to God's prompting as we interact with others. Anchored in persevering prayer, we speak scriptural truths into the lives of others as the Holy Spirit leads. Like the unveiling of a beautiful bride at her wedding, the spiritual veil is removed and Christ's truth and goodness are revealed.

Made in USA - North Chelmsford, MA
1360304_9781649603463
02.13.2023 1555